How to Use

History Pockets
My Portfolio

W9-BBD-530

In *History Pockets—Native Americans,* students learn about eight different Native American tribes from the Arctic to the southeastern United States. The engaging activities are stored in labeled pockets and bound into a decorative cover. Students will be proud to see their accumulated projects presented all together. At the end of the book, evaluation sheets have been added for teacher use.

Make a Pocket

1. Use a 12" x 18" (30.5 x 45.5 cm) piece of construction paper for each pocket. Fold up 6" (15 cm) to make a 12" (30.5 cm) square.

2. Staple the right side of each pocket closed.

3. Punch two or three holes in the left side of each pocket.

Assemble the Pocket Book

1. Reproduce the cover illustration on page 3 for each student.

2. Direct students to color and cut out the illustration and glue it onto a 12" (30.5 cm) square of construction paper to make the cover.

3. Punch two or three holes in the left side of the cover.

4. Fasten the cover and the pockets together. You might use string, ribbon, twine, raffia, or binder rings.

Every Pocket Has...

Overview Page
This teacher reference page describes the activities presented in each pocket.

Pocket Label, Shelter Stamp, Picture Dictionary Cards
Reproduce the page for students. As each tribe is studied, direct students to color and cut out the pocket label and glue it onto the pocket. Instruct students to color and cut out the shelter stamp and glue it onto the map of Native American tribes on page 8. Have students follow the directions on page 10 for using the picture dictionary cards.

Pocket Label

Shelter Stamp

Picture Dictionary Cards

Teacher Fact Sheet
Use this background information as a reference for the activities presented in the pocket.

Student Booklet
Reproduce the pages to make an information booklet for each student. Staple the booklet to a 9" x 12" (23 x 30.5 cm) piece of construction paper for durability.

Activities
Have students do the activities and store them in the labeled pocket.

NATIVE AMERICANS

THE INUIT
OF THE ARCTIC

THE SIOUX
OF THE PLAINS

THE TLINGIT
OF THE NORTHWEST

THE NAVAJO
OF THE SOUTHWEST

THE NEZ PERCE
OF THE PLATEAU

THE IROQUOIS
OF THE NORTHEAST

THE MAIDU
OF CALIFORNIA

THE SEMINOLE
OF THE SOUTHEAST

Name Georgia

Pocket 1 • **INTRODUCTION TO**

NATIVE AMERICANS

CUT AND PASTE

Pocket Label...................................... page 5

See page 2 for information on how to prepare the pocket label and shelter stamp. See page 10 for information on how to prepare the picture dictionary cards.

FACT SHEET

Tribes of North America .... page 6

Read this background information to familiarize yourself with the tribes of North America. Share the information with your students as appropriate. Incorporate library and multimedia resources that are available.

ACTIVITIES

Map and Chart of Native American Tribes........................... pages 7–9

Two ongoing activities help students learn about maps and charts. Students locate the regions of the Native American tribes, and then look for the similarities and differences among the tribes.

Make a Picture Dictionary .... pages 10 & 11

Students create a picture dictionary of new words and Native American terms found throughout the book. Use the activity to preview vocabulary before the unit or to reinforce vocabulary throughout the unit. A list of dictionary words and definitions are included for teacher reference on page 94.

NATIVE AMERICANS

© Evan-Moor Corp.• EMC 3703

NATIVE AMERICANS

© Evan-Moor Corp.• EMC 3703

Pocket Labels

FACT SHEET
TRIBES OF NORTH AMERICA

The name "Native Americans" describes the people who lived in America when Christopher Columbus and other Europeans arrived. Many books use the name "American Indians." There were at least 600 tribes of Native Americans scattered across North America during the 1500s. To study the wide range of different Native Americans, it is common to divide them among geographic regions. Those regions include the Arctic, the Subarctic, the Northwest Coast, California, the Plateau, the Great Basin, the Southwest, the Great Plains, the Northeast, and the Southeast. Within each region, there were many different tribes. Each of these tribes, however, had its own heritage, customs, and values. The types of shelters they made and the kinds of food they ate depended on the natural resources available to them in the region.

One major tribe from 8 of the 10 regions is included in this book.

REGION	TRIBE
Arctic	**Inuit**
Northwest Coast	**Tlingit**
Plateau	**Nez Perce**
California	**Maidu**
Great Plains	**Sioux**
Southwest	**Navajo**
Northeast	**Iroquois**
Southeast	**Seminole**

It is important to remember that Native Americans are not merely part of the past. There are 2.5 million Native Americans, representing 500 tribes, living in the United States and Canada today. They live and work in cities, suburbs, rural areas, and on reservations. There are still hundreds of reservations located across the United States, but less than half the total population of Native Americans live on them. Native Americans are citizens of the United States and also their tribal nations. As well as acculturating into the larger society, Native Americans also take great pride in reviving tribal traditions and customs. Throughout the world, Native Americans are known for their deep appreciation of the land and their dedication to its preservation.

MAP ANSWER KEY FOR PAGE 8

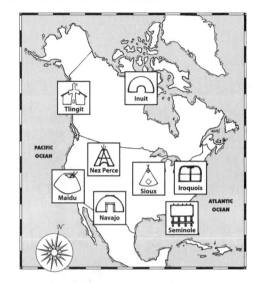

CHART ANSWER KEY FOR PAGE 9

TRIBE	CLOTHING	FOOD	SHELTER
Inuit	parka, mittens, boots	seal, walrus, whale, fish, polar bear, caribou	igloos
Tlingit	animal skin pants, leather aprons, nose rings	salmon, sea lion, otter, goat, deer, elk, bear	plank houses with totem poles
Nez Perce	buckskin shirts and dresses, leggings, breechcloths, moccasins, cornhusk hats	roots, berries, seeds, salmon, deer, elk, moose, bear, sheep, goat, buffalo, small animals	longhouses, underground shelters and tipis
Maidu	breechcloths, grass skirts, grass caps	fish, elk, small animals, seeds, acorns, roots	earth lodges
Sioux	animal skin shirts, leggings, breechcloths, fringed dresses, moccasins	buffalo, berries, roots, herbs, wasna	tipis
Navajo	deerskin breechcloths, leggings, dresses, moccasins	corn, potatoes, wheat, fruit, sheep, fry bread	hogans
Iroquois	deerskin breechcloths, leggings, skirts, moccasins	corn, beans, squash, maple syrup, fish, deer, moose, acorns	longhouses
Seminole	cotton shirts, blouses, skirts, breechcloths, leggings	corn, beans, squash, fish, alligator, deer, bear, raccoon, squirrel, birds, roots, potatoes	chickees

MAP AND CHART OF NATIVE AMERICAN TRIBES

The Native Americans covered in this book lived in eight different regions. One major tribe from each region is presented with focus on its clothing, food, shelter, and daily life. The following activities help students to compare and contrast the eight different tribes.

STEPS TO FOLLOW

How to Use the Map of Native American Tribes

1. Distribute the map of North America from page 8 to students. Talk about where the eight tribes are located.

2. Tell students that as they study each of the tribes, they are going to color and cut out the shelter stamp from the "Cut and Paste" page in each pocket. Then they will glue the stamp in the appropriate map square.

3. Using the information on the teacher fact sheet, discuss the geographical features of the region and the type of shelter used by that particular tribe.

4. Repeat the same procedure as each tribe is studied.

5. Store the map in Pocket 1.

Note: A completed map is provided on page 6 for reference.

How to Use the Comparison Chart of Native American Tribes

1. Distribute two copies of the comparison chart from page 9 to each student. Tell students they are going to compare and contrast the clothing, food, and shelter of the tribes.

2. As each tribe is studied, fill in the chart using the information from the teacher fact sheet and student booklet pages for reference.

3. When the whole chart is complete, discuss the similarities and differences between the clothing, food, and shelters of the tribes.

4. Store the comparison chart in Pocket 1.

Note: A completed comparison chart is provided on page 6 for reference.

MATERIALS

- page 8 and two copies of page 9, reproduced for each student
- shelter stamp from each tribe, reproduced (with the "Cut and Paste" pages) for each student
- pencil
- crayons
- scissors
- glue

Name: _____

MAP OF

NATIVE AMERICAN TRIBES

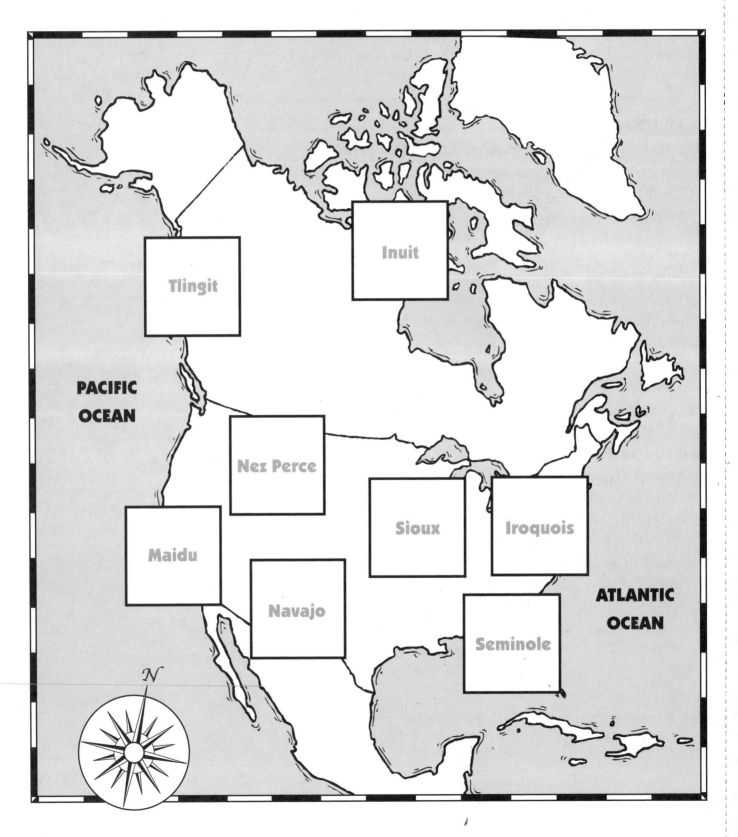

EMC 3703 • *Native Americans* • © Evan-Moor Corp.

COMPARISON CHART OF
NATIVE AMERICAN TRIBES

TRIBE	CLOTHING	FOOD	SHELTER
Inuit			
Tlingit			
Nes			

MAKE A PICTURE DICTIONARY

Create a picture dictionary of words and terms from the Native American tribes studied in this book. The blank dictionary forms are provided on page 11. Pictures for clothing, food, and shelter for each tribe are found on the "Cut and Paste" page of each pocket. Words and definitions for all the tribes are provided for teacher reference on page 94.

STEPS TO FOLLOW

1. Tell the students that they will keep a picture dictionary of words they learn as they study Native Americans.

2. Have students cut the blank picture dictionary forms apart. They will have 24 pages all together.

3. Punch a hole in the corner of the dictionary pages and the construction paper.

4. Bind the pages together with a construction paper front and back, using a binder ring or large fastener. You may choose to have students add a string of beads as an additional decoration.

5. Decorate the front cover.

6. Keep the dictionary in the "Introduction" pocket.

7. As you begin the study of each tribe, add its three picture squares to the dictionary.

   a. Color and cut out the pictures of clothing, food, and shelter, and other items.

   b. Glue each picture onto a dictionary page.

   c. Write a definition for each word.

MATERIALS

- page 11, six copies reproduced for each student
- scissors
- two 4" x 5" (10 x 13 cm) pieces of colored construction paper
- glue
- hole punch
- binder ring or large fastener
- crayons or marking pens
- Optional: string and beads

MAKE A PICTURE DICTIONARY

Pocket 2

THE INUIT
OF THE ARCTIC

CUT AND PASTE

**Pocket Label, Shelter Stamp,
Picture Dictionary Cards**................... **page 13**
See page 2 for information on how to prepare the
pocket label and shelter stamp. See page 10 for
information on how to prepare the picture
dictionary cards.

FACT SHEET

The Inuit...................................... **page 14**
Read this background information to familiarize
yourself with the Inuit. Share the information with
your students as appropriate. Incorporate library
and multimedia resources that are available.

STUDENT BOOKLET

Make an Inuit Booklet .... **pages 15–17**
See page 2 for information on how to prepare the
student booklet. Read and discuss the information
as a class. Encourage students to read their booklets
to partners or independently.

ACTIVITIES

Arctic Ice Fishing .... **pages 18 & 19**
There's nothing "fishy" happening when you set
students free to go ice fishing like the Inuit.

Tell Me a Story.......................... **pages 20–22**
Ask students to imagine they are tucked away
warmly inside their igluviaks and let them share
stories Inuit-style.

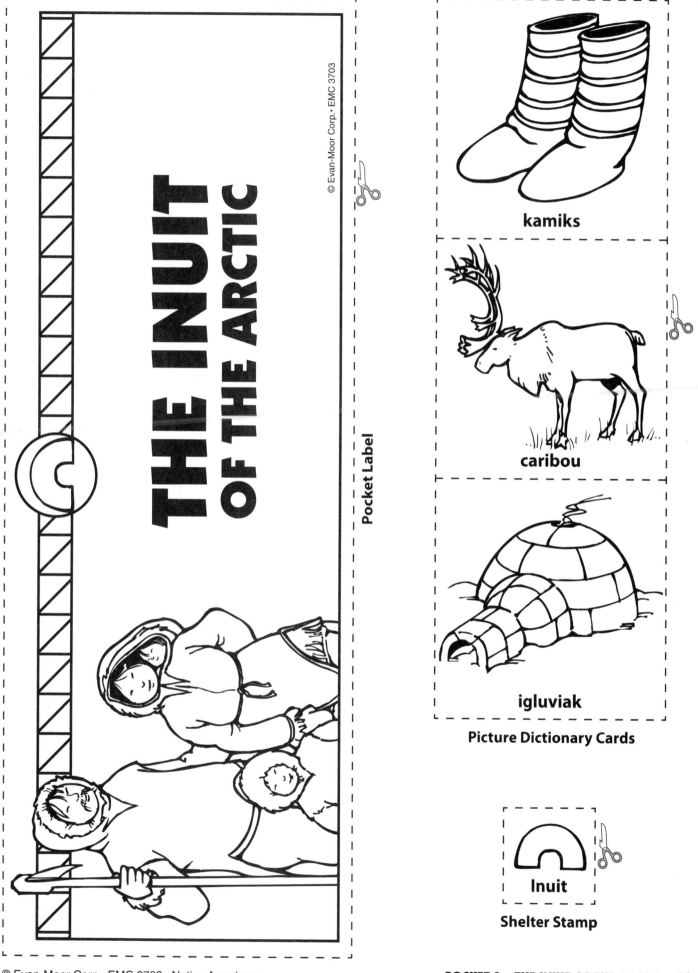

THE INUIT OF THE ARCTIC

Pocket Label

kamiks

caribou

igluviak

Picture Dictionary Cards

Inuit

Shelter Stamp

FACT SHEET
THE INUIT

INTRODUCTION

Many Native American groups lived in the Arctic. The Inuit (IHN yoo iht) people were one group who called this region their home. The Inuit inhabited the Northwest Territories, Greenland, and Alaska. The word *Inuit* is an Eskimo word that means "The People." Many neighboring groups called the Inuit "Eskimos," but this name is not correct. The term *Eskimo* means "Eaters of Raw Meat." Although the Inuit did eat raw meat, the name was meant as an insult.

CLOTHING

The Inuit wore special clothing to keep them dry and warm in the freezing temperatures. Their clothing was made of many layers, so that air trapped between the layers would keep their bodies warm.

Inuit men, women, and children wore the same types of clothing. The Inuit wore pants made from white bearskin. Each person also wore a heavy fur coat made from fox, seal, or caribou. Underneath their heavy coats, Inuit people wore shirts made from bird skin. They wore lightweight, waterproof parkas over their coats to keep themselves dry.

Every Inuit wore a pair of mittens made from sealskin or caribou. Each mitten often had two thumbs. Sometimes a person's thumb got wet and cold. When this happened, it was easy to turn the mitten around and use the other thumb covering without taking off the mitten.

Each family member wore a pair of boots called kamiks. The kamiks were made from sealskin. Even the huskies wore little skin shoes to protect their paws from the cold arctic weather.

When the sun's rays reflected off the snow, there was often a blinding glare. This made it difficult for the Inuit to see. The Inuit wore special goggles. They made the goggles from wood or bone. They cut a small hole in the center of each eyepiece so that the person wearing them would be able to see.

FOOD

The very cold temperature and climate of the tundra made growing crops impossible for the Inuit. Inuit men spent most of their time hunting and ice fishing. Often the Inuit ate raw seal, caribou, walrus, whale, and fish.

Sometimes they preserved the meat so they could eat it later. To preserve the meat, they placed it in bags made from dried meat or whale blubber. The Inuit also ate fish and blood soup.

SHELTER

The Inuit called their homes igloos. An igloo was not just a snow- or ice-covered house, though. The Inuit built three different types of igloos: sod houses, snow houses, and tents.

Sod houses were the most permanent types of homes. The bottom of the house was made out of sod. Whalebone and driftwood were used to build the sides and roof. Sod was then packed onto the igloo to keep it insulated.

Inuit families often had to leave their sod houses to move farther out onto the ice. There they could hunt and fish more easily. While on the ice, the Inuit lived in snow-covered igloos called igluviaks. The Inuit built their igluviaks from blocks of hard, frozen snow. A block of ice in the ceiling served as a skylight.

When winter was over, the snow-covered igloos began to melt. Then the Inuit moved away from the ice fields and built tents from wooden poles and animal skins. The Inuit knew where caribou and other animals would arrive in the spring. These were the areas where the Inuit set up their tents.

FAMILY LIFE

Inuit children, parents, and other relatives lived in one shelter. Inuit families spent a great deal of time indoors because of the harsh weather. They told stories, played string games, made soapstone carvings, and sang songs.

Boys trained at an early age to become hunters like their fathers. Harpoons, kayaks, and dogsleds were important tools. Boys also learned how to build snow houses and make weapons.

Girls learned how to make new clothing, repair old clothing, set traps, and trim wicks. Both boys and girls were taught how to train dogs and drive a sled.

EMC 3703 • Native Americans • © Evan-Moor Corp.

THE INUIT
OF THE ARCTIC

The Inuit have lived in the far north Arctic areas for a long time. The Arctic is a cold and frozen area. Greenland, Canada, and Alaska are places where the Inuit live. Some people call these Native Americans "Eskimos." They like the name "Inuit" better.

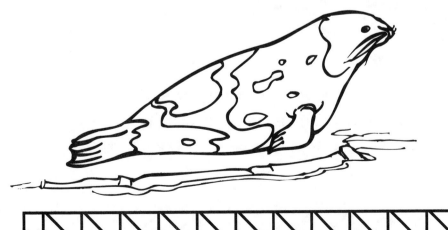

Inuit men, women, and children wore special clothing to keep them warm. Shirts were made from bird skins. Pants and coats were made from animal fur. They wore lightweight parkas over their clothing. The parkas were waterproof to keep their clothing dry. The Inuit also wore mittens and boots, called **kamiks**. Even the dogs wore skin shoes to keep their paws dry and warm.

The Inuit were not able to grow crops. The weather was too cold. The Inuit hunted and fished for food. Inuit men used their harpoons and kayaks to hunt seal, walrus, whale, and fish. Sometimes they cut a hole in the ice and waited for a fish to bite. On land they hunted polar bear and **caribou**.

The Inuit lived in snow houses called **igluviaks**. They were built out of blocks of hard snow. In the spring, the igluviaks melted. Then the Inuit moved to where the caribou lived. They built tents from wooden poles and animal skins. When the long winter returned, the Inuit made snow houses again.

Inuit children, parents, and other relatives lived in one shelter. The Inuit spent much of their time indoors. They often told stories, sang songs, carved soapstone, and played string games. Boys learned how to build snow houses and hunt. Girls learned how to make clothing and set traps. Both boys and girls learned how to drive a sled and care for dogs.

▶ **Inuit men used their harpoons and kayaks to hunt seal, walrus, whale, and fish.**

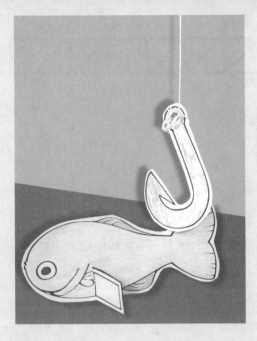

ARCTIC ICE FISHING

The Inuit often cut a hole in the ice, dropped their hook and line into the water, and waited. Invite students to go ice fishing Inuit-style by making a fish and pole. Then let the patience and fun begin!

MATERIALS

- page 19, reproduced for each student
- plastic drinking straw
- 36" (91.5 cm) length of string
- two 1" (2.5 cm) magnet strips
- marking pens
- scissors
- hole punch
- 9" x 12" (23 x 30.5 cm) tagboard
- masking tape
- glue

STEPS TO FOLLOW

1. Color the hook and fish parts on page 19.

2. Glue the page to a piece of tagboard and cut out the parts. Carefully cut the slits in both the fish and the strip.

3. Using a hole punch, make a hole through the circle at the top of the fishhook.

4. Thread the string through the straw. Knot one end of the string and wrap masking tape around the knot. Make sure the masking tape "ball" is large enough to keep the string from pulling back through the straw.

5. Tie the other end of the string through the hole at the top of the hook.

6. Peel off the adhesive strip on the back of each magnet strip. Stick one magnet onto the fish where an eye should be. Stick the other magnet in the center of the hook.

7. To make the fish stand upright, fit the strip and the bottom of the fish together. Slide both parts together on the slits as shown.

8. Stand the fish upright on the floor. Pull on the string until the hook is at the top of the straw. Slowly lower the hook and try to make the two magnet pieces touch.

9. Tell students to get ready to reel in their fish. Have students think about what it would feel like to sit on the ice and wait for a fish to take the bait. You may choose to have students write a brief description of what they would see, hear, and feel.

Step 7

ARCTIC ICE FISHING

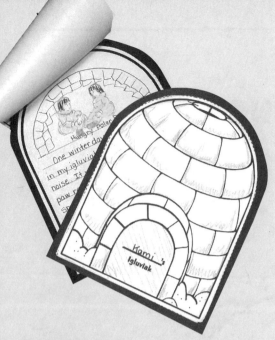

TELL ME A STORY

What did the Inuit do to entertain themselves during long winters? Why, tell stories, of course. The Inuit spent long periods telling stories and passing down oral traditions while they sat together inside their igluviaks. Invite students to pass the time by creating stories to share just like the Inuit.

MATERIALS

- pages 21 and 22, reproduced for each student
- 9" x 12" (23 x 30.5 cm) black construction paper
- scissors
- stapler
- crayons
- pencil

STEPS TO FOLLOW

1. Discuss what it would be like to be an Inuit living on the tundra. On page 22, each student writes a personal experience about something that may have happened on the tundra. (More mature writers may need several copies of page 22.)

2. Draw and color pictures of children tucked away inside the igluviak at the top of the writing form.

3. Cut out both igluviak patterns.

4. Staple the patterns together so that the story pattern is behind the cover pattern. Glue the story pattern to black construction paper, trimming around the edges.

5. Have students write their name on the cover pattern. Lift the top page and share the Inuit story.

EMC 3703 • Native Americans • © Evan-Moor Corp.

TELL ME A STORY

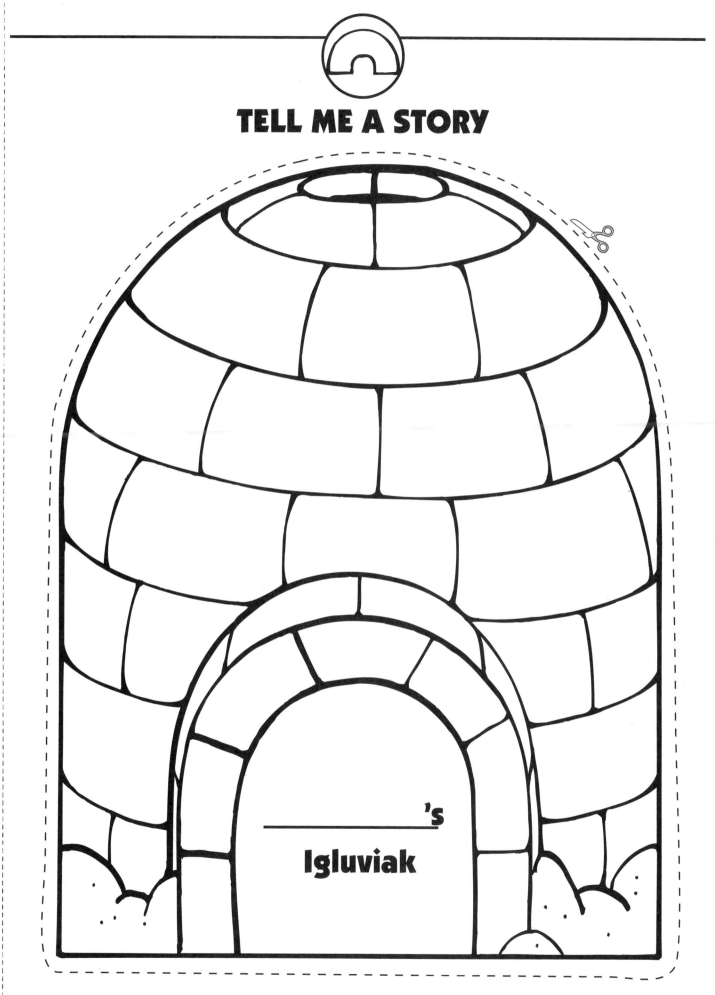

_____'s
Igluviak

TELL ME A STORY

Pocket 3

THE TLINGIT
OF THE NORTHWEST

CUT AND PASTE

**Pocket Label, Shelter Stamp,
Picture Dictionary Cards**................... **page 24**
See page 2 for information on how to prepare the
pocket label and shelter stamp. See page 10 for
information on how to prepare the picture
dictionary cards.

FACT SHEET

The Tlingit.................................... **page 25**
Read this background information to familiarize
yourself with the Tlingit. Share the information
with your students as appropriate. Incorporate
library and multimedia resources that are
available.

STUDENT BOOKLET

Make a Tlingit Booklet................. **pages 26–28**
See page 2 for information on how to prepare the
student booklet. Read and discuss the information
as a class. Encourage students to read their booklets
to partners or independently.

ACTIVITIES

Create a Potlatch Mask .... **pages 29 & 30**
Going to a potlatch is a special event. Students make a
raven potlatch mask to wear to a potlatch celebration.

Totem Pole Layer Book .... **pages 31 & 32**
What is the meaning behind a totem pole? Students
will find out when they create their own Tlingit
totem pole layer books.

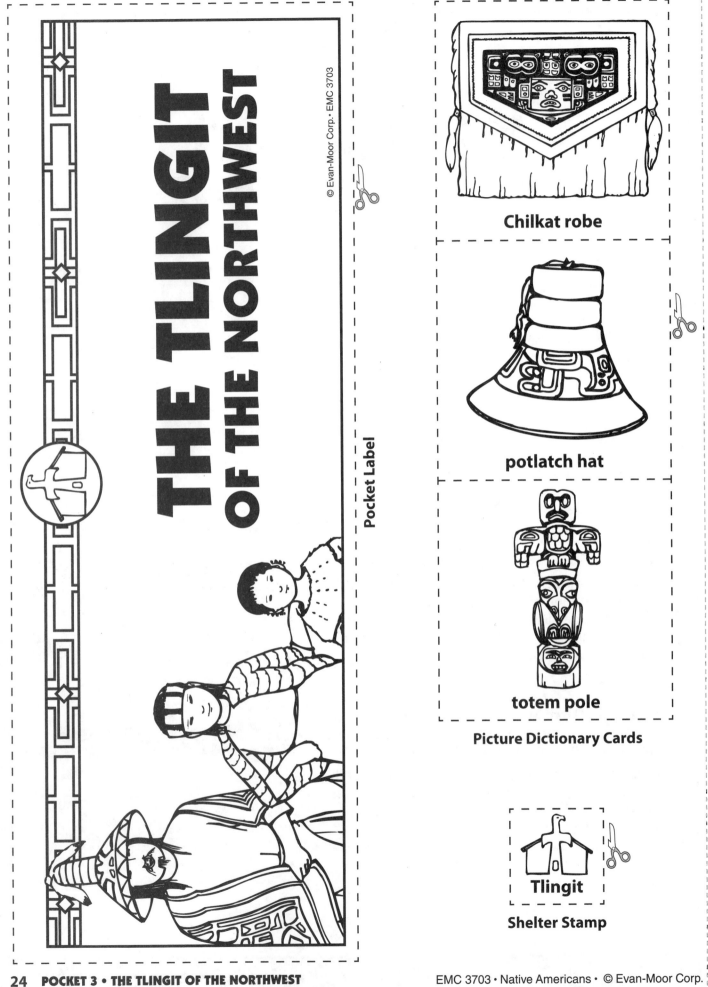

THE TLINGIT OF THE NORTHWEST

© Evan-Moor Corp. • EMC 3703

Pocket Label

Chilkat robe

potlatch hat

totem pole

Picture Dictionary Cards

Tlingit

Shelter Stamp

FACT SHEET
THE TLINGIT

INTRODUCTION

One of many Native American groups that lived along the Northwest Coast was the Tlingit (KLIHN kiht). The Tlingit made their home along the southeastern coast of Alaska, northern British Columbia, and the Yukon Territory. The Northwest Coast was rich in natural resources. Food was plentiful, and the Tlingit often had more food than they needed. They often traded their excess food with neighboring tribes in return for other goods.

CLOTHING

The Tlingit wore animal skin pants with feet in them, leather aprons, and skin blankets made from rabbits or marmots. Men and women wore nose rings and earrings. Some people pierced their lower lips and wore tattoos.

The Tlingit had ceremonial clothing for special feasts called potlatches. They wore carved masks, potlatch hats, dancing dresses, and Chilkat robes. Chilkat robes could be fur-trimmed, multicolored, or fringed. Chilkat robes and dancing dresses had extreme value. The animal designs on the masks, hats, and clothing identified the person's clan.

FOOD

The most important source of food for the Tlingit was salmon. In early spring, millions of salmon would swim from the salty Pacific Ocean to freshwater rivers to lay their eggs. The Tlingit called this event the salmon run. The salmon run lasted from spring until late summer. It was not unusual for a family to catch more than 1,000 pounds (454 kilograms) of salmon during a salmon run. A large portion of the salmon was dried or smoked so it could be preserved for future meals.

Each summer and fall, the Tlingit people lived in fishing camps near the sea. They built large canoes and caught halibut and other types of fish, sea lions, and otters. On the shore, they gathered clams and mussels. Near the forests, the Tlingit hunted animals such as goat, deer, elk, and bear.

In the winter, the Tlingit held ceremonial potlatches. Potlatches were often held to honor the dead or celebrate good fortune. People often ate seal meat, fish, berries, and vegetables at a potlatch. Guests ate and ate until they became sick, which was considered a great compliment to the family who hosted the potlatch. Potlatches could often last up to 12 days. Many potlatches took years to plan.

SHELTER

The Tlingit built large plank houses. They used red and yellow cedar, yew, alder, maple, and Sitka spruce from the vast Northwest coastal forests. Many times, planks were cut from large trees without chopping down the trees.

As winter approached, the Tlingit left their fishing camps. During winter several families lived together in one house. The Tlingit painted their houses with bright pictures and colorful designs. The designs usually depicted animals and birds. Common raven family crests included raven, whale, salmon, and frog. Eagle crests included eagle, bear, shark, and thunderbird. The Tlingit often carved these animal crests on the beams, doorways, and entrances of their homes. Many wealthy families had elaborately carved panels in the interior of the house.

Huge wooden totem poles stood in front of each home. Tlingit families recorded their family histories by carving special animals and birds on the totem poles. Most totem poles were 40 to 60 feet (12 to 18 meters) tall, but some measured more than 100 feet (30 meters). Raising a totem pole was a special event. Totem poles were often raised at potlatches.

FAMILY LIFE

Each plank house was home to several families who belonged to the same clan. The relationships were established through the mother's side of the family. When a boy reached eight years old, he went to live with his mother's brother. There he eventually learned to hunt game animals, as well as other responsibilities. Girls learned house traditions from their mothers and grandmothers. Both boys and girls learned from their elders the clan's history and customs.

THE TLINGIT
OF THE NORTHWEST

The Tlingit have lived along the Northwest Coast of North America for a long time. This area includes Alaska and Canada. The Tlingit lived near forests, rivers, and the Pacific Ocean. They traveled in canoes to trade fish, shells, furs, carvings, and woven blankets.

The Tlingit wore animal skin pants, leather aprons, and skin blankets. Men and women wore nose rings and earrings. Some Tlingit people pierced their lower lips and wore tattoos. The Tlingit had special clothing that they wore to feasts called potlatches. At potlatches, the Tlingit wore carved masks, **potlatch hats**, dancing dresses, and robes called **Chilkat robes**.

A fish called salmon was the most important food for the Tlingit. In early spring, millions of salmon swam from the ocean to the rivers to lay their eggs. The Tlingit called this the salmon run. During a salmon run, a family could catch more than 1,000 pounds (454 kilograms) of salmon. The Tlingit also ate other types of fish, sea lion, and otter. They gathered clams and mussels from the shores. They hunted goat, deer, elk, and bear in the forests.

The Tlingit built large plank houses. They used cedar, maple, and spruce trees to build their houses. The Tlingit painted their houses with bright pictures and colorful animal designs. These designs stood for a family's clan. Huge wooden **totem poles** stood in front of each home. The Tlingit carved animal symbols on the totem poles to tell the history of their families.

Each plank house was home to several families. The families belonged to the same clan. When a boy reached eight years old, he went to live with his mother's brother. His uncle taught him how to hunt game animals. Mothers and grandmothers taught girls how to weave blankets and make baskets. The Tlingit used storytelling to pass down their history to both boys and girls.

CREATE A POTLATCH MASK

The Tlingit made clan masks to wear to special potlatch celebrations. Encourage students to celebrate Tlingit-style by making a raven clan crayon-resist mask.

STEPS TO FOLLOW

1. Talk about the potlatch celebration as described on page 27 of the student booklet. Remind students that decorative masks, hats, and clothing were worn for this special occasion.

2. Have students color and cut out the raven mask on page 30.

3. Direct students to glue the mask onto black construction paper, trimming around the edges.

4. Instruct students to punch three holes in the mask. Then they thread raffia through each of the holes and tie it.

5. Have students tape a wood dowel to the back of the mask. Now it is ready for the potlatch celebration.

MATERIALS

- page 30, reproduced for each student
- 9" x 12" (23 x 30.5 cm) black construction paper
- crayons or marking pens
- scissors
- glue
- transparent tape
- hole punch
- raffia
- 12" (30.5 cm) wood dowel, stick, or ruler

CREATE A POTLATCH MASK

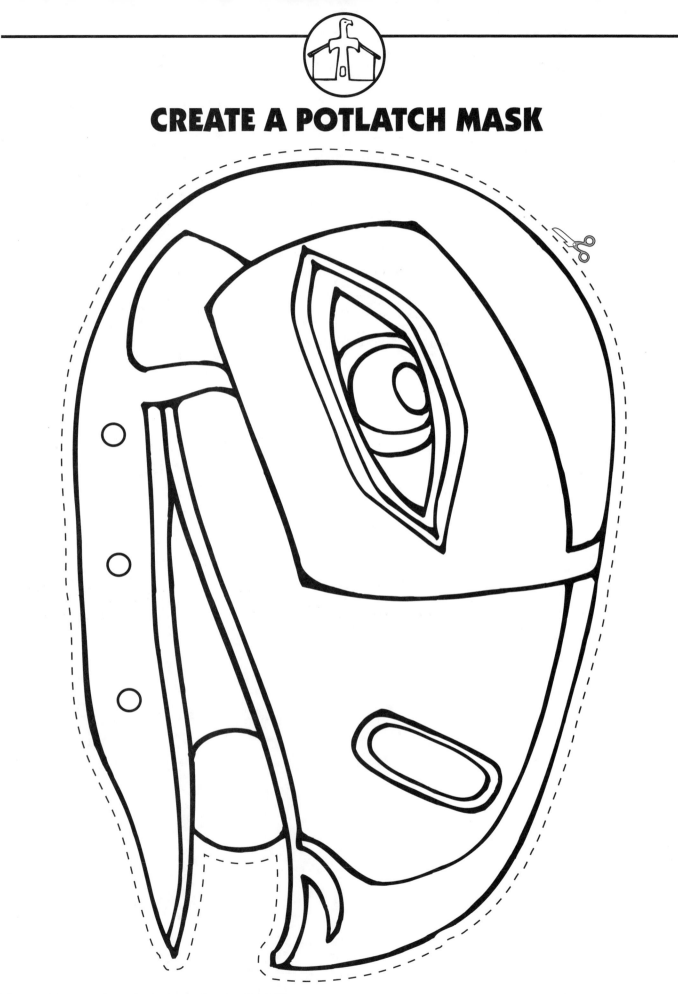

TOTEM POLE LAYER BOOK

The Tlingit carved animal symbols on totem poles to help them tell their family histories. Encourage students to create their own totem pole layer books to tell about their families.

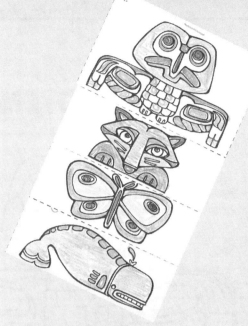

STEPS TO FOLLOW

1. As a class, make a list of the qualities of the four animals represented in the totem pole book on page 32. For example: The raven is smart, free-spirited, and independent. The fox is shy, clever, and fast. The butterfly is delicate, colorful, and beautiful. The whale is strong, friendly, and a good swimmer.

2. Have students cut apart the four totem pole layers.

3. Assemble the layers in the proper order (from shortest on top to longest on the bottom).

4. Staple the book together at the top.

5. Have students choose four people in their family that they think have the same qualities as the four animals in the book.

6. Direct students to lift the raven picture and write about a person who is like the raven. The students then lift the fox picture and write about a person who is like the fox. Then they lift the butterfly picture and write about a person who is like a butterfly at the top of the page and about a person who represents the whale at the bottom of the page.

7. Have students color the four animals and then share the totem pole layer books with the class.

MATERIALS

- page 32, reproduced for each student
- stapler
- scissors
- crayons
- pencil

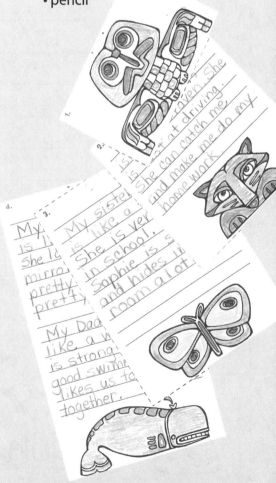

Pocket 4

THE NEZ PERCE
OF THE PLATEAU

CUT AND PASTE

Pocket Label, Shelter Stamp,
Picture Dictionary Cards................... **page 34**
See page 2 for information on how to prepare the
pocket label and shelter stamp. See page 10 for
information on how to prepare the picture
dictionary cards.

FACT SHEET

The Nez Perce .... **page 35**
Read this background information to familiarize
yourself with the Nez Perce. Share the information
with your students as appropriate. Incorporate
library and multimedia resources that are
available.

STUDENT BOOKLET

Make a Nez Perce Booklet .... **pages 36–38**
See page 2 for information on how to prepare the
student booklet. Read and discuss the information
as a class. Encourage students to read their booklets
to partners or independently.

ACTIVITIES

Create an Appaloosa Ornament..... **pages 39 & 40**
The Appaloosa horse was important to the Nez Perce.
Students make an Appaloosa ornament, and then
write three ways horses were valuable to the Nez
Perce.

Chief Joseph, Nez Perce Leader ..... **pages 41 & 42**
Chief Joseph is considered one of the greatest
leaders in history. Students write adjectives on feathers
to describe what makes a good leader.

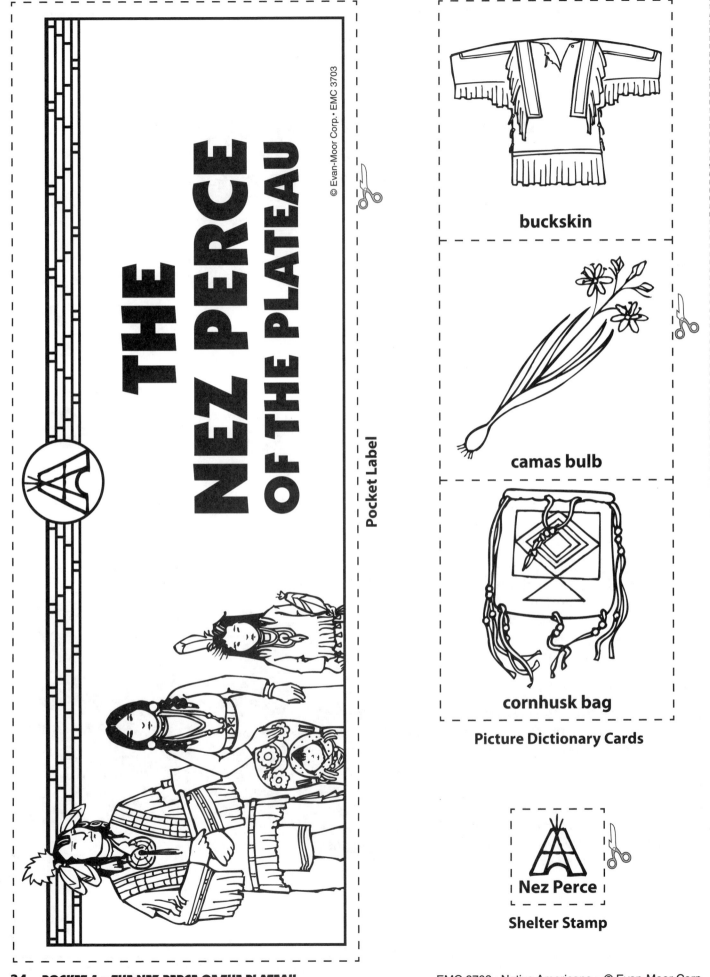

© Evan-Moor Corp. • EMC 3703

Pocket Label

THE NEZ PERCE OF THE PLATEAU

buckskin

camas bulb

cornhusk bag

Picture Dictionary Cards

Nez Perce

Shelter Stamp

FACT SHEET
THE NEZ PERCE

INTRODUCTION

The Nez Perce (nehz PURS) lived in the Plateau region of the United States. Their original territory covered the canyon areas of the Snake, Clearwater, and Salmon Rivers of Oregon, Washington, and Idaho. Now most live in Idaho. The tribe officially called themselves "Nimi'ipuu" (The People). The French renamed them "Nez Perce," which means "pierced nose." A French interpreter gave the name to the group after he saw some of them wearing shells in their noses for decoration. Few of these Native Americans ever pierced their noses, but the tribe is still known today as the Nez Perce.

CLOTHING

The Nez Perce men and boys wore long, fringed buckskin shirts and leggings. They also wore belts, breechcloths, and moccasins. Feathered bonnets were also common for men to wear. During colder weather, men put on bison skin robes and gloves.

Women and girls wore long, belted buckskin dresses and knee-length moccasins. Their dresses were decorated with items such as elk teeth, beads made of shell and bone, and porcupine quills. Women used vegetable and mineral dyes to make clothes colorful. They also wore cornhusk basketry hats. Nez Perce women carried their babies on their backs in cradleboards. Cradleboards were made of thick twigs and a covering of soft animal skin adorned with beads.

FOOD

The foods gathered and the game hunted varied with the seasons. In the spring, women traveled to valleys to dig root crops. These roots included camas bulbs, bitterroot, wild carrot, and wild potato. They gathered berries such as gooseberries, thorn berries, and currants. Women collected pine nuts, seeds, and black moss.

In the summer, the people moved the village higher in the mountains to set up temporary camps. Here the people gathered more roots, fished the streams for salmon, and hunted big game. Men hunted deer, elk, moose, bear, mountain sheep, and goat. They traveled by horse to the Montana plains to hunt buffalo and antelope. The men also hunted small game like rabbit, squirrel, badger, marmot, and ruffed grouse.

By late fall, the Nez Perce moved back into their traditional villages. Here they prepared for the long winter by drying and preserving foods.

SHELTER

Part of the year, the Nez Perce lived in longhouses called kuhetini-t (koo-HAT-in-eet). The longhouse had a wooden frame covered with woven tule mats. Tule is a marsh plant found near rivers and streams. Some longhouses were over 100 feet (30 meters) long. There were several rows of hearths in the center for families to cook their meals.

A circular semisubterranean sweathouse, a woman's monthly seclusion hut, and a submerged hot bath were also part of the village.

When the Nez Perce moved about, they erected wali-mini-ts (wahl-LEE-min-eets) made of tule mats or buffalo skins. These were similar to the tipis of the Plains tribes.

FAMILY LIFE

Several related, extended families made up a Nez Perce village. A headman led each village. He was a respected elder who was often the shaman. A shaman is the religious leader and healer.

Nez Perce men made bows from the horns of mountain sheep. Boys developed good hunting skills early. Men trained and bred Appaloosa horses. The Nez Perce became known as experts in horse-riding skills.

Men spent the winter playing games and telling stories to the young. Men played vigorous team sports to prepare them for hunting big game. The stories imparted sacred traditions and practical knowledge to the children of the tribe.

Women taught girls the traditional skills of cooking, weaving, and basketry. The cornhusk bags that women wove from hemp fiber were important for daily use and for trade.

Ceremonies were held to assure good harvests. Music and dance were central to the ceremonies. People played rattles, drums, and flutes. There were ceremonial songs and chants for births, marriages, deaths, hunting, and for war.

THE NEZ PERCE
OF THE PLATEAU

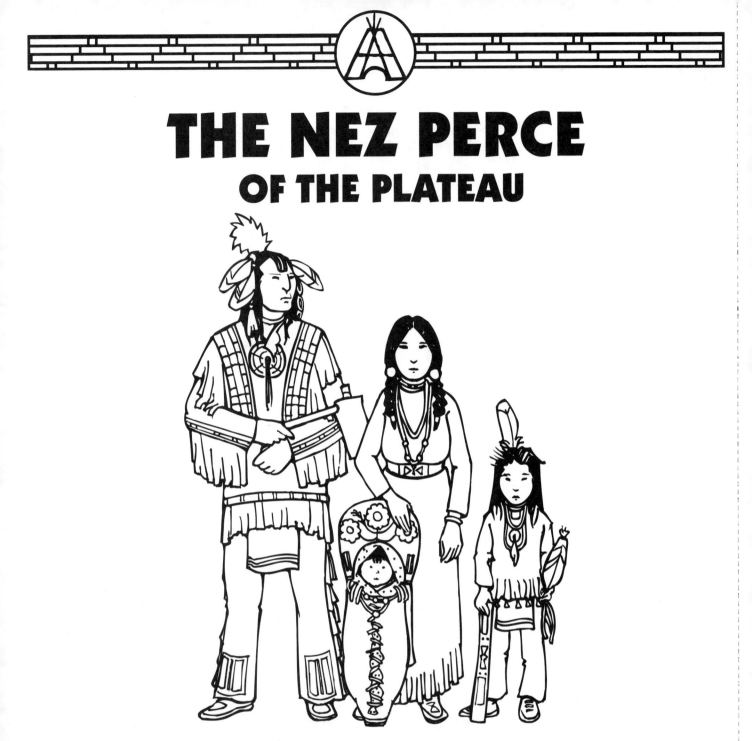

The Nez Perce have lived in the Plateau region of North America for a long time. The Plateau region is in Oregon, Washington, and Idaho. The area has mountains, forests, grasslands, and rivers. The tribe called themselves Nimi'ipuu. This means "The People." The French called the tribe Nez Perce. **Nez Perce** means "pierced nose" in French. They did not really pierce their noses. Some of the men did wear shells in their noses for decoration. The tribe decided to keep the name Nez Perce.

EMC 3703 • Native Americans • © Evan-Moor Corp.

▶ **Women used vegetable and mineral dyes to make clothes colorful. People decorated their clothing with beads, porcupine quills, and elk teeth.**

The Nez Perce wore buckskin clothing. **Buckskin** is another word for deerskin. Men and boys liked long, fringed shirts and leggings. They wore belts, breechcloths, and moccasins. The women and girls wore long, belted buckskin dresses. They wore cornhusk hats on their heads and knee-length moccasins on their feet. Sometimes the people put on gloves and buffalo skin robes to keep warm in the winter.

The Nez Perce hunted and fished for their food. The men hunted big game such as deer, elk, moose, bear, mountain sheep, and goat. The men used Appaloosa horses to hunt buffalo and antelope. Boys were taught to hunt rabbit, squirrel, badger, and marmot. The men and boys fished for salmon. The women and girls gathered roots. Their favorite roots to eat were the **camas bulb** and bitterroot. They collected pine nuts, seeds, and black moss. The girls liked to gather all kinds of berries. During the winter, the people spent time drying and storing all the food.

▶ **Their favorite roots to eat were the camas bulb and bitterroot.**

The Nez Perce lived in different kinds of homes. Most of the year, they lived in tipis made of woven tule mats or buffalo skins. Tule is a plant that grows near rivers. The Nez Perce could take their shelter with them as they looked for food. They lived in longhouses in the winter. The longhouse was over 100 feet (30 meters) long and was made of poles and tule mats. Several families lived together in a longhouse. They also had an underground hot bath and sweathouse for ceremonies near the longhouse.

The Nez Perce lived in villages along streams and rivers. Several related families lived together in one village. Men did the hunting, using bows and arrows. Men trained spotted horses called Appaloosas. Men and boys played sports games. The men told stories to the children. The women taught girls cooking, weaving, and basketry. They made beautiful **cornhusk bags**. Everyone in the village enjoyed ceremonies. They danced and chanted to music made from rattles, drums, and flutes.

CREATE AN APPALOOSA ORNAMENT

The horse was important to Native Americans. The Nez Perce were considered the best equestrians in the Northwest. They trained and bred Appaloosas. These spotted horses were greatly valued because they could move swiftly into battle, outrun buffalo, and carry supplies. To show their importance, Appaloosas were adorned with beautiful blankets, harnesses, and beaded ornaments that were worn on their foreheads.

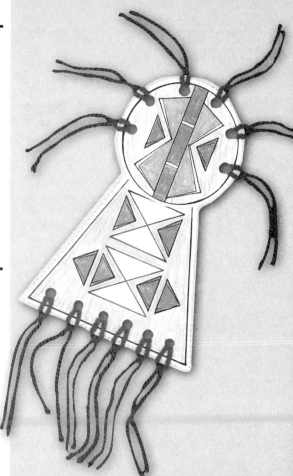

STEPS TO FOLLOW

1. Color the patterns on page 40, using earth colors.

2. Cut out the patterns for the ornament and glue them onto tagboard to make them stronger. Cut around the glued patterns to make two pieces.

3. Use a hole punch to make 6 holes on both the top and bottom pieces.

4. Put glue where indicated on the triangular piece. Overlap the circular piece. Allow glue to dry.

5. Thread and tie 8" pieces of yarn in the 12 holes around the ornament.

6. Tie feathers and beads to the ornament, if desired.

7. On the back of the ornament, write three ways Appaloosas helped the Nez Perce. (For example, they moved swiftly into battle, outran buffalo, and carried supplies.)

MATERIALS

- page 40, reproduced for each student
- 9" x 12" (23 x 30.5 cm) tagboard
- crayons
- twelve 8" (20 cm) pieces of yarn, twine, raffia, or ribbon
- scissors
- glue
- hole punch
- Optional: feathers and beads

CREATE AN APPALOOSA ORNAMENT

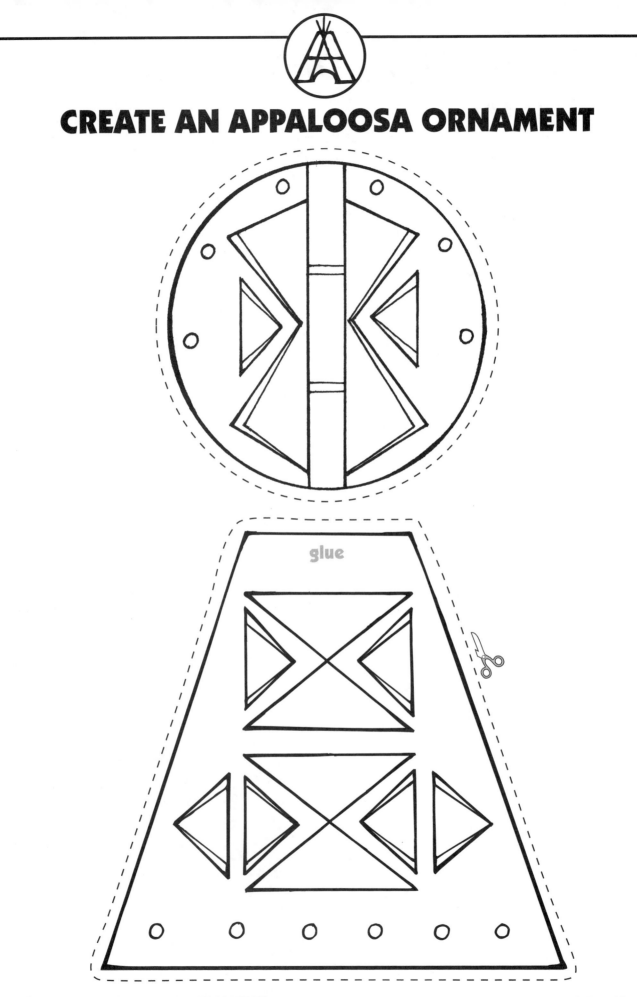

glue

EMC 3703 • Native Americans • © Evan-Moor Corp.

CHIEF JOSEPH, NEZ PERCE LEADER

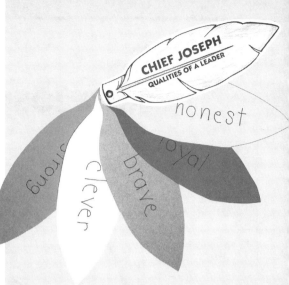

Chief Joseph has been called one of the greatest Native American leaders. His real name was Hinmaton Yalatikit (Thunder-that-comes-from-the-mountain). In 1877 the U.S. government told the Nez Perce they had to move from their beloved hunting grounds to a small reservation in Idaho. The Nez Perce refused to go to the reservation. Instead they decided to go to Canada to live. Chief Joseph led 800 people on a 1,800-mile (2,896 km) journey, always being pursued by soldiers. Time after time, Chief Joseph's outnumbered warriors fought off the cavalry. Finally, only 40 miles (64 km) from the Canadian border, soldiers ambushed the Nez Perce. Chief Joseph decided to save the 418 survivors (87 men, 184 women, and 147 children) by surrendering. He faced the soldiers and said these famous words: "I will fight no more forever." Chief Joseph spent the next 27 years championing the human rights of his people. He will always be remembered for his great leadership, spirit, strength, and courage.

STEPS TO FOLLOW

1. Discuss the importance of Chief Joseph and the qualities that made him a great leader of his people. Utilize reference materials appropriate for your students.

2. Make a list of adjectives to describe a good leader (strong, trustworthy, smart, brave, loyal, polite, powerful, likeable, respectful, hardworking, honest, patient, curious, clever, daring, caring, etc.).

3. Have students color and cut out the cover feather on page 42. Have them glue it to the red construction paper, trimming around the edges.

4. Direct students to cut out the other feather and use it as a template to make five feathers in the remaining colors of construction paper.

5. Have students write a word that describes Chief Joseph on each of the five feathers.

6. Instruct students to punch a hole at the bottom of each feather.

7. Have students gather all the feathers together, putting the cover feather on top. Put a paper fastener through the holes.

8. Fan out the feathers to read about the qualities of a good leader.

MATERIALS

- page 42, reproduced for each student
- 4" x 9" (10 x 23 cm) strips of construction paper—one of each: red, blue, yellow, brown, green, and white
- crayons
- marking pens
- scissors
- paper fastener
- hole punch

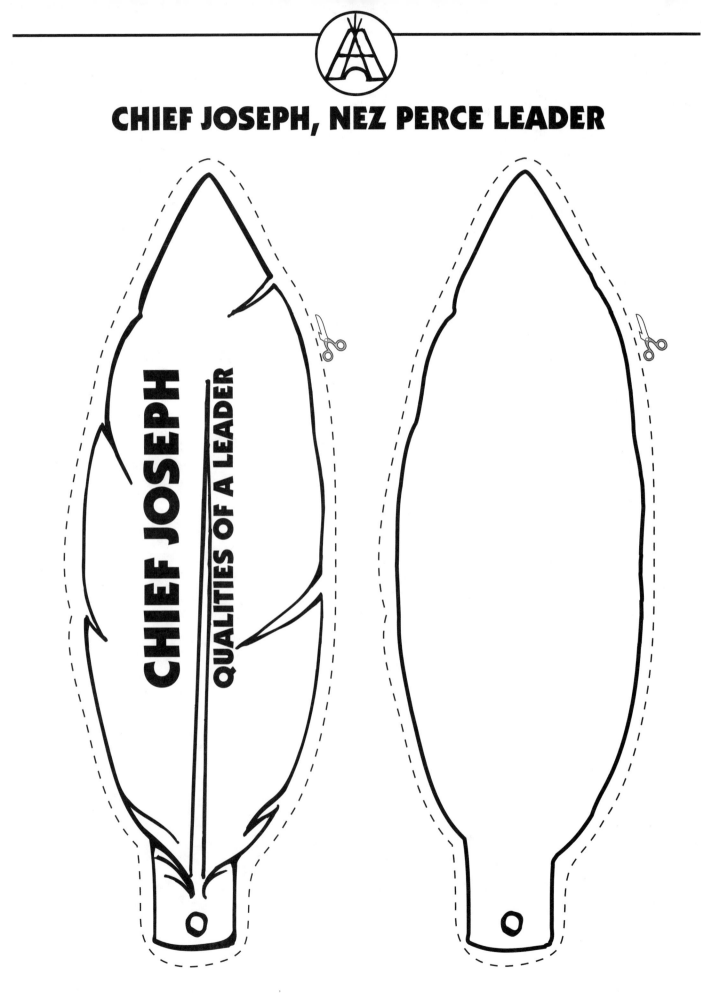

CHIEF JOSEPH

QUALITIES OF A LEADER

Pocket 5

THE MAIDU
OF CALIFORNIA

CUT AND PASTE

**Pocket Label, Shelter Stamp,
Picture Dictionary Cards**.................... **page 44**
See page 2 for information on how to prepare the
pocket label and shelter stamp. See page 10 for
information on how to prepare the picture
dictionary cards.

FACT SHEET

The Maidu .... **page 45**
Read this background information to familiarize
yourself with the Maidu. Share the information
with your students as appropriate. Incorporate
library and multimedia resources that are
available.

STUDENT BOOKLET

Make a Maidu Booklet .... **pages 46–48**
See page 2 for information on how to prepare the
student booklet. Read and discuss the information
as a class. Encourage students to read their booklets
to partners or independently.

ACTIVITIES

Maidu Seed Beater..................... **pages 49–51**
The Maidu used seed beaters to knock seeds from
their stalks. Students follow simple directions to
create seed beaters.

Bear Rattle and Chant................ **pages 52 & 53**
Liven up the classroom by having students make
Maidu-style bear rattles. The class then creates
a bear chant to use with the rattles.

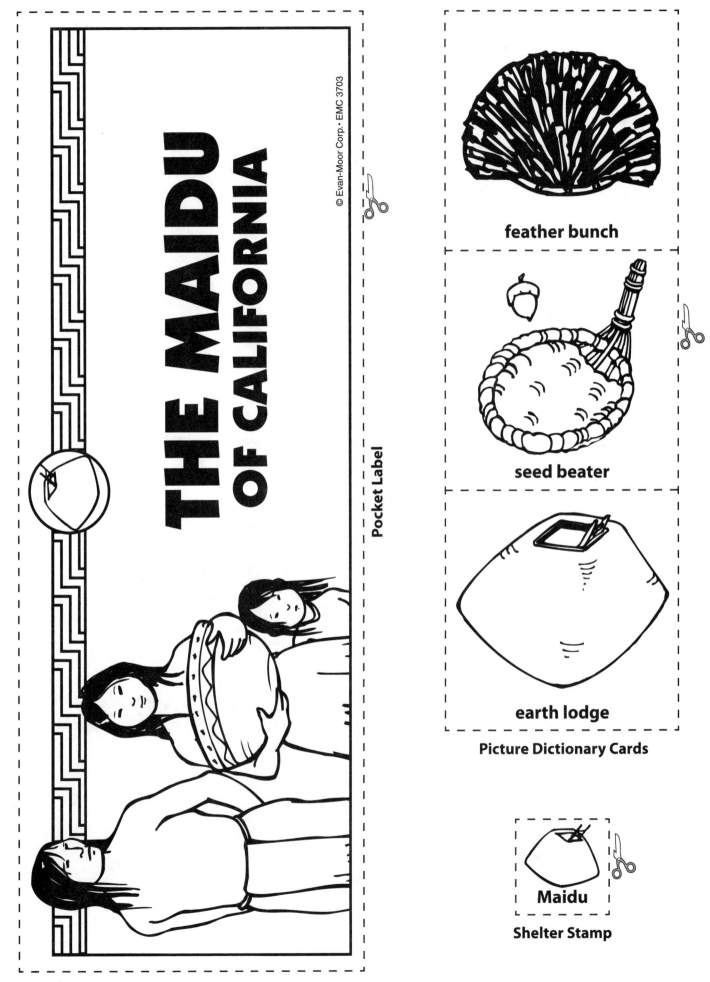

© Evan-Moor Corp. • EMC 3703

THE MAIDU OF CALIFORNIA

Pocket Label

feather bunch

seed beater

earth lodge

Picture Dictionary Cards

Maidu

Shelter Stamp

FACT SHEET
THE MAIDU

INTRODUCTION

Long ago, the land we know today as California was home to more than 60 small Native American tribes. One of these tribes, the Maidu (MY doo), roamed the fertile coastal lands, wooded hills, and river valleys of this region.

The Maidu called themselves "Maydi," which meant "human beings"; however, they used this word to include every living thing. The word *Maidu* is actually a European word that means "Digger Indians," because the Maidu often dug roots to supplement their diet.

CLOTHING

The Maidu wore very little clothing because of the warm climate. Men wore breechcloths, short skirts made from grass, or nothing at all. Some men wore their hair long; others wore it short. The Maidu did not use knives to cut their hair, though. Instead, they used hot coals and ashes to burn away the hair they wanted to remove.

Women wore long bone and wooden earrings decorated with feathers. They also wore caps made from river grasses. Around their waists, women wore aprons made from strips of bark or grass. Some women wore moccasins, while others preferred to go barefoot.

The Maidu wore special clothing for ceremonies. Women wore feather bunches, or dance plumes, on their heads. The feather bunches were made of quills, feathers, wood, and string. Men often wore feather crowns.

FOOD

The Maidu did not farm. They preferred to hunt and gather. The Maidu ate fish they caught from the ocean and rivers. They also hunted deer, elk, rabbit, squirrel, and birds. However, most of their diet consisted of seeds, acorns, and roots. The acorns were ground into flour and used to make bread or to thicken soup and porridge.

The village chief decided when Maidu men should hunt deer. If a Maidu killed a deer or any other living thing, they gave something back to the animal by dancing, praying, or singing.

SHELTER

Maidu homes were rounded earth lodges made from wood, earth, branches, and twigs. Next to each earth lodge, the Maidu built a barrel-shaped container in which they stored acorns and other seeds.

The Maidu lived in small villages surrounding one large village. Each small village consisted of many families. The villages faced south so that the Maidu could benefit from the constant rays of the warm sun. The Maidu always set up their villages near fresh running water, usually a nearby stream or river.

FAMILY LIFE

Maidu women were very skilled at making tightly-woven baskets. These baskets could hold a number of things—even water. The women made baskets from bark, grasses, twigs, and cattails. The Maidu used these baskets to gather seeds, store food, rock babies, and for hats. Each basket showed great workmanship and detail. No two baskets looked the same.

Small children and girls helped the Maidu women collect seeds and dig roots. They used seed beaters to knock the seeds off their tall stems. Then they collected the seeds in their baskets and trays. Girls also learned how to cook, tan hides, and make baskets.

The men of the tribe taught the boys how to fish and hunt. When a Maidu boy turned 15, he was admitted to the men's secret Kuksu society. For several days, a celebration occurred. When it was over, the boy was considered a man.

The Maidu participated in ceremonies, such as the Bear Dance. This ceremony included singing, dancing, and feasting. One tribe member pretended to be the bear. The person wore a bearskin and acted out the part of a hungry bear searching for food. Maidu children then chased after the bear with willow branches until the bear grew tired of running away. At this point, the bear gave a signal and singing, dancing, and praying began.

THE MAIDU
OF CALIFORNIA

The Maidu roamed the wooded hills and river valleys of the land we know today as California. The Maidu called themselves "Maydi," which means "human beings." The Maidu were one of more than 60 Native American tribes that lived in California.

The Maidu wore very little clothing. Men wore breechcloths and short grass skirts. Some men wore their hair long, while others cut it short. The Maidu used hot coals and ashes to burn away the hair they did not want. Women wore aprons made from grass or bark. They wore caps woven from river grasses. Both men and women wore **feather bunches** at ceremonies.

The Maidu did not farm. They hunted and gathered their food. The Maidu caught and ate fish from the ocean and rivers. The village chief decided when the Maidu men should hunt deer. The men also hunted elk, rabbit, squirrel, and birds. The Maidu liked to eat seeds and roots. Their favorite food was acorns. The acorns were ground into flour and used to make bread or to thicken soup.

The Maidu built rounded homes made from wood, dirt, branches, and twigs called **earth lodges**. Next to each home was a barrel-shaped container used to store acorns and other seeds. A small Maidu village might have 15 people in it. A large village could have hundreds of people. The Maidu set up their villages near streams or rivers so they could have fresh water.

Maidu women and girls made baskets from bark, grasses, twigs, and cattails. They collected seeds in baskets called **seed beaters**. Girls learned how to cook and make clothes from animal skins. Maidu men taught the boys of the tribe how to fish and hunt. When a boy turned 15, the Maidu had a celebration. After the celebration, the tribe treated the boy as a man. The Maidu had other celebrations, such as the Bear Dance.

EMC 3703 • Native Americans •

MAIDU SEED BEATER

The Maidu made seed beaters to help them collect seeds for their meals. While walking in the fields, the Maidu beat the tall grass stalks with their woven seed beaters and collected the seeds in their baskets. Invite students to make seed beaters and then use them on a walk in a grassy field.

STEPS TO FOLLOW

1. Talk about how seed beaters were made and their use.

2. On the pattern on page 50, have students write a sentence about the seed beater.

3. Have students color both seed beater patterns.

4. Direct students to glue each pattern to a piece of cardboard and cut them out.

5. Have students staple the left sides of the seed beater together, leaving the top and bottom ends open as shown.

6. Instruct students to glue craft sticks to the handle of the seed beater as shown.

MATERIALS

- pages 50 and 51, reproduced for each student
- two 9" x 12" (23 x 30.5 cm) pieces of cardboard or tagboard
- crayons
- scissors
- craft sticks (5 per student)
- stapler
- glue

Steps 5 & 6

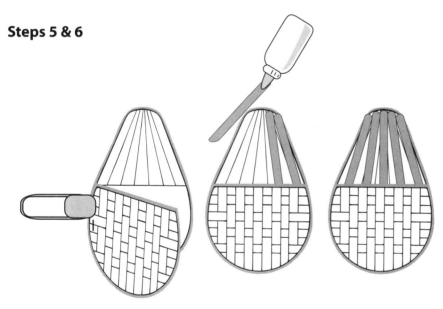

MAIDU SEED BEATER

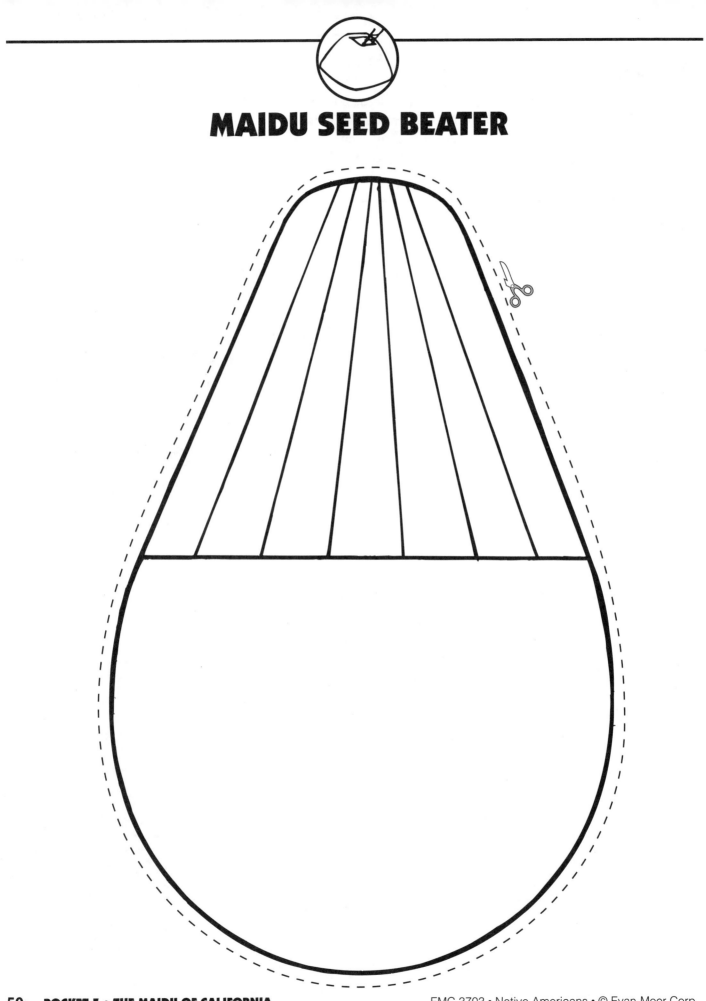

EMC 3703 • Native Americans • © Evan-Moor Corp.

MAIDU SEED BEATER

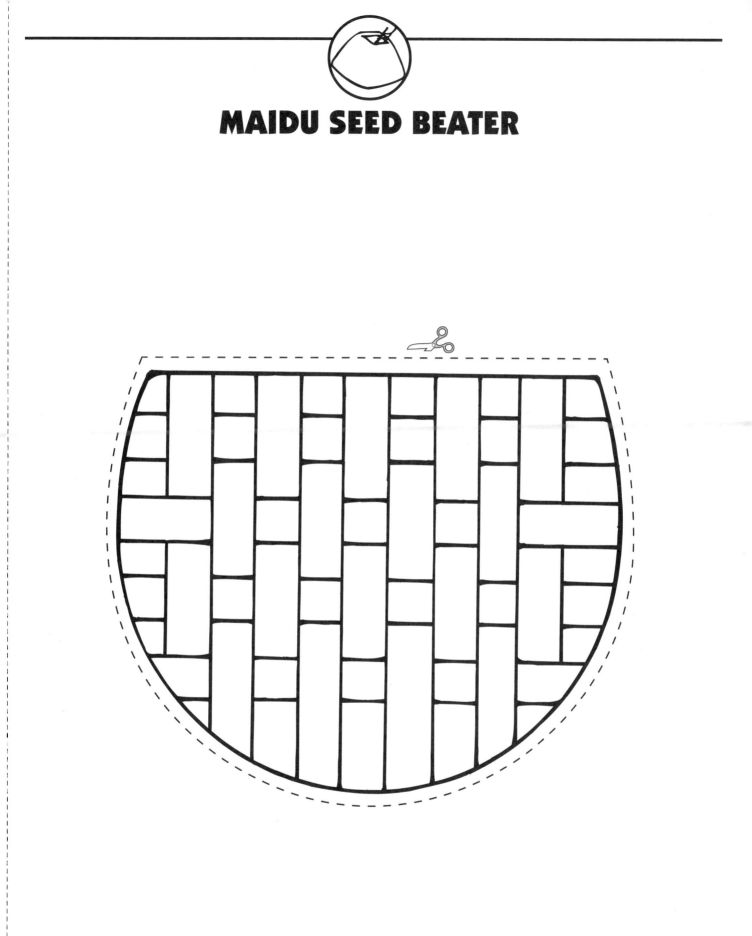

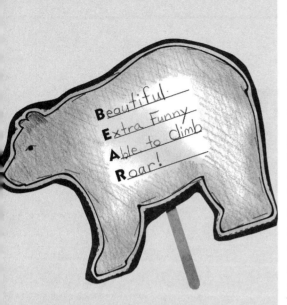

BEAR RATTLE AND CHANT

The Maidu had a celebration called the Bear Dance. One person played the hungry bear waking up from a long winter's nap. Children chased the bear. Others formed a big circle around the bear and children. People then started dancing and singing. The bear led all the people in a parade to a nearby stream. The people wore garlands and chanted along the way. As they paraded, the people made as much noise as possible. When they reached the stream, everyone washed their faces and threw the garlands into the water. This symbolized the throwing away of all bad feelings and the beginning of new love and friendship.

Invite students to make a bear rattle, create a class chant, and then participate in a Maidu Bear Dance.

MATERIALS

- page 53, reproduced for each student
- two 9" x 12" (23 x 30.5 cm) pieces of construction paper
- craft stick
- transparent tape
- crayons
- dried beans
- stapler
- pencil

STEPS TO FOLLOW

1. Use page 53 to write words that describe a bear. Make sure that the words begin with the letter shown at the beginning of each line.

2. Color and cut out the bear.

3. Glue the bear to a sheet of construction paper.

4. To make the front of the rattle, cut around the bear shape, leaving a border of construction paper.

5. Place the front of the rattle on the second sheet of construction paper and trace around it to make the back of the rattle.

6. Cut out the back of the rattle.

7. Staple the two pieces of the rattle together around the edges, leaving a space open at the bottom.

8. Place a handful of dried beans inside the rattle and staple the open space closed so the beans will not fall out.

9. Securely tape a craft stick to the bottom backside of the rattle.

10. The class then can make up a chant about a bear coming out of hibernation.

11. Shake the rattle and chant away!

EMC 3703 • Native Americans • © Evan-Moor Corp.

BEAR RATTLE AND CHANT

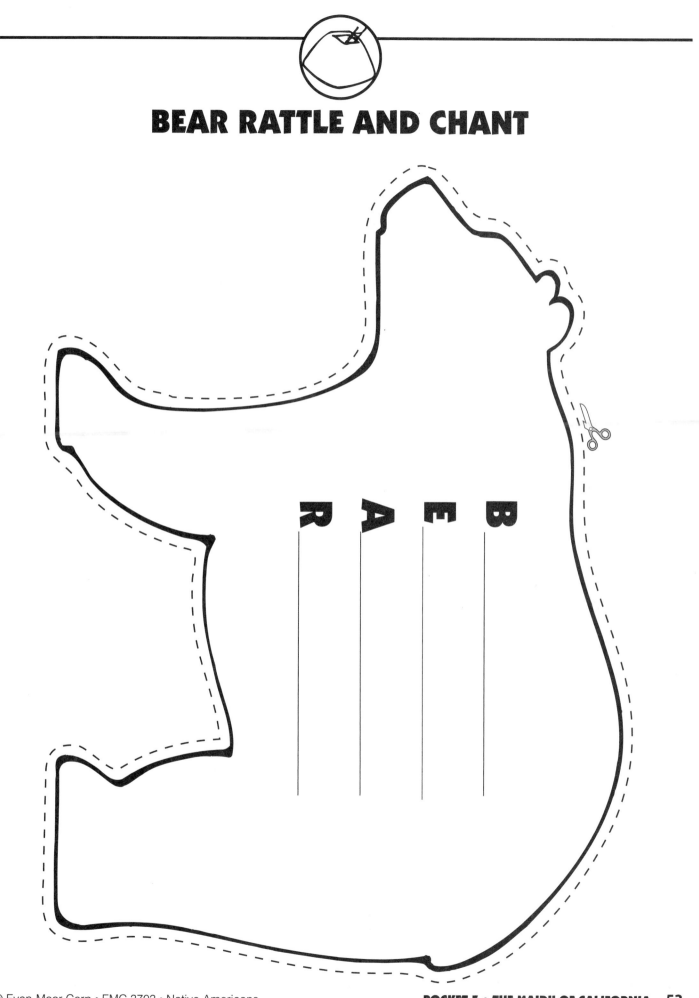

R A E B

Pocket 6

THE SIOUX
OF THE PLAINS

CUT AND PASTE

Pocket Label, Shelter Stamp,
Picture Dictionary Cards.................... **page 55**
See page 2 for information on how to prepare the pocket label and shelter stamp. See page 10 for information on how to prepare the picture dictionary cards.

FACT SHEET

The Sioux...................................... **page 56**
Read this background information to familiarize yourself with the Sioux. Share the information with your students as appropriate. Incorporate library and multimedia resources that are available.

STUDENT BOOKLET

Make a Sioux Booklet.................. **pages 57–59**
See page 2 for information on how to prepare the student booklet. Read and discuss the information as a class. Encourage students to read their booklets to partners or independently.

ACTIVITIES

The Amazing Buffalo .... **pages 60–62**
The Sioux depended greatly on the buffalo. Students make booklets showing some of the uses for this incredible beast.

Ceremonial Ankle Band..................... **page 63**
This beaded ankle band is perfect to wear when dancing at ceremonies.

THE SIOUX
OF THE PLAINS

© Evan-Moor Corp. • EMC 3703

Pocket Label

parfleche

wasna

tipi

Picture Dictionary Cards

Sioux

Shelter Stamp

THE SIOUX

INTRODUCTION

The Sioux (SOO) roamed the plains of North America from as far north as present-day Wisconsin and Canada to as far south as present-day Texas. The Sioux Nation encompasses fourteen bands, which make up three main tribes: Lakota, Nakota, and Dakota.

CLOTHING

Most Sioux clothing was made from buffalo hide and other animal skins. The skins were tanned and dyed with natural pigments using berries, leaves, grasses, and flowers. Sioux women sewed the hides together using needles of sharpened bone. They also used buffalo sinew (tendons) to make tough, durable thread.

Women wore fringed dresses decorated with porcupine quills, horsehair, fox tails, and beads. Many of these same materials were used to make jewelry. Men wore fringed shirts and breechcloths. In the winter, they wore fur robes and leggings. Men also wore blankets or soft robes made from fox or wolf skins. Both men and women wore moccasins. The Sioux also made parfleches out of rawhide. A parfleche was a folded rawhide envelope that was used to hold food or something special.

FOOD

The buffalo provided the Sioux with their main source of food. They often cooked the meat in a bowl made from the buffalo's stomach. Because the stomach was pliable, it was easy to stretch the stomach muscle across a wooden frame. The Sioux also dried buffalo meat so they would have meat for the winter when buffalo were scarce.

Women and children gathered berries, wild turnips, roots, and herbs. Berries were often dried and stored in containers made from buffalo hide. The turnips were peeled, dried, and pounded into flour. The turnip flour was then used to thicken broth that was flavored with wild herbs.

The Sioux also ate wasna. Wasna was made from lean meat that the women dried and pounded into fine particles. The meat particles were then mixed with melted fat and crushed berries. Similar to beef jerky, wasna was especially easy to eat while hunting or traveling. Wasna was often stored in parfleches.

SHELTER

The word *tipi* comes from two Sioux words meaning "an object used to live in." The Sioux were able to assemble and disassemble their tipis so they could follow the roaming buffalo across the plains.

A tipi was constructed with large lodgepoles that measured about 20 feet (6 meters) in length. Then the women scraped, tanned, and sewed a dozen buffalo hides together to make the tipi covering. The Sioux decorated their tipis with a variety of ceremonial symbols. When the weather was hot, the tipi covering was rolled up on the sides to allow for more air circulation.

An average-size tipi could sleep six people. Bedding was rolled up in the morning to make room for daily activities. Weapons were kept on the men's side of the tipi, while cooking pots and utensils were kept on the women's side. When it was time to move, the women disassembled the tipi and loaded it onto a travois, which acted as a sled and could easily be pulled by a horse.

FAMILY LIFE

Men made all the decisions for the tribe, and one man was chosen as chief. While women were not involved in decision-making, they had great influence over their husbands and often made suggestions about what should be done.

Women owned all family belongings. Young Sioux children played together near the women. Girls played with miniature tipis and dolls made from animal hide. Boys often pretended to hunt with small bows and arrows.

When children reached the age of five or six, they learned adult skills. Sioux women taught girls to cook, tan hides, make clothing, and assemble tipis. Boys were taught how to hunt and become great warriors. They also learned how to care for horses and often participated in hunting activities. Both boys and girls were responsible for taking care of the younger children.

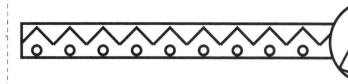

THE SIOUX
OF THE PLAINS

The Sioux roamed the plains of North America in search of buffalo. They went as far north as Wisconsin and Canada. They traveled as far south as Texas. The Sioux Nation was made up of three main tribes: Lakota, Nakota, and Dakota.

Sioux clothing was made from buffalo hide and other animal skins. The skins were dyed many different colors. The Sioux used berries, leaves, grasses, and flowers to make the dyes. Sioux women wore fringed dresses. They decorated their clothes with porcupine quills, horsehair, and beads. Men wore fringed shirts and breechcloths. In the winter, they wore fur robes and leggings. Both men and women wore moccasins.

Buffalo was the main food for the Sioux. They ate fresh buffalo meat. They also dried and stored meat for the winter. The Sioux used meat to make **wasna**, a kind of beef jerky. The meat was dried and pounded into small pieces. Then it was mixed with crushed berries and melted fat. The wasna was stored in a **parfleche** bag. Women and children also gathered berries, roots, herbs, and wild turnips.

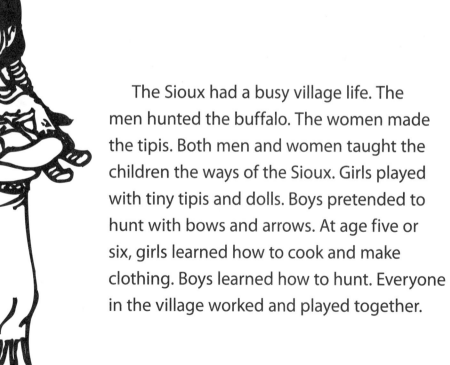

The Sioux lived in **tipis** that were easy to put together and take apart. They could take their home with them when they followed the buffalo. They put the tipi on a kind of sled called a travois. Sioux women sewed many buffalo hides together to make the tipi covering. They used buffalo sinew (tendons) as thread. Then it was decorated with symbols. When the weather was hot, the tipi covering was rolled up on the sides. A tipi could hold six people.

The Sioux had a busy village life. The men hunted the buffalo. The women made the tipis. Both men and women taught the children the ways of the Sioux. Girls played with tiny tipis and dolls. Boys pretended to hunt with bows and arrows. At age five or six, girls learned how to cook and make clothing. Boys learned how to hunt. Everyone in the village worked and played together.

THE AMAZING BUFFALO

To the Native Americans of the Great Plains, the buffalo was a walking commissary. This animal provided them with 70 different items for food, clothing, and shelter. Students make a booklet showing some of the uses for this incredible beast.

- pages 61 and 62, reproduced for each student
- 9" x 12" (23 x 30.5 cm) tan construction paper (or use brown wrapping paper)
- scissors
- glue
- crayons

STEPS TO FOLLOW

1. As a class, read and discuss the information about the buffalo. Bring in additional sources of information as desired.

2. Fold the construction paper in half.

3. Color the buffalo on page 61, cut on the dotted lines, and then glue it to the front of the folded construction paper.

4. Open the folded construction paper. Cut out and glue the information in the box to the inside top half of the folder.

5. Cut out and glue the two labeled boxes on page 62 to the bottom half of the folder.

6. Cut apart the pictures of the items made from the buffalo.

7. Glue them in the correct boxes.

THE AMAZING BUFFALO

The buffalo is also called the American bison. A large male buffalo could be 12 feet (almost 4 meters) long from head to tail and up to 6 feet (2 meters) tall. He could weigh as much as 2,000 pounds (900 kilograms).

At one time, millions of buffalo roamed the Great Plains of North America. A herd could be so large that it would take several days to pass by!

Native Americans used the buffalo for food, shelter, and clothing. All parts of the buffalo were used—skin, hair, bones, horns, flesh, and tendons (called sinew). Nothing was wasted.

THE AMAZING BUFFALO

BONES AND HORNS	HIDE AND SINEW

tipi cover **whistle** **needle** **scoop** **moccasins** **knife**

scraper **bow string** **buffalo robe** **shirt** **shield** **arrowhead**

EMC 3703 • *Native Americans* • © Evan-Moor Corp.

ANKLE BAND

Sioux women sewed beautiful beadwork of many colors to decorate war shirts, dresses, moccasins, leggings, and other pieces of clothing. Heavily beaded clothing was used for ceremonies. It was common to add bells to beaded ankle bands for dancing.

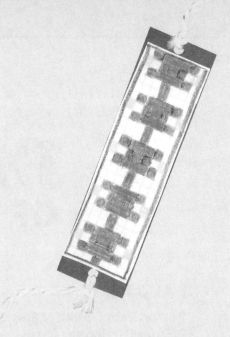

STEPS TO FOLLOW

1. If possible, show students pictures of the beadwork that is representative of the Sioux. Then have students color a pattern on the graph paper to represent the beadwork on the ankle bands.

2. Students glue the colored graph paper pattern to the brown construction paper.

3. After the glue is dry, students make a black crayon line around the graph paper.

4. Students punch a hole on each end of the ankle band.

5. Students thread a piece of yarn or string through the holes and then tie the strings together to hold the band around the ankle.

6. Optional: Students may thread bells to the yarn before tying. Students wear the ankle bands and dance to the music of drums and flutes.

MATERIALS

- 1¾" x 6" (4 x 15 cm) quarter-inch graph paper

- 2" x 7" (5 x 18 cm) brown construction paper

- two 7" (18 cm) pieces of yarn or string

- crayons or marking pens

- glue

- hole punch

- Optional: small bells and Native American music (flutes and drums)

Pocket 7

THE NAVAJO
OF THE SOUTHWEST

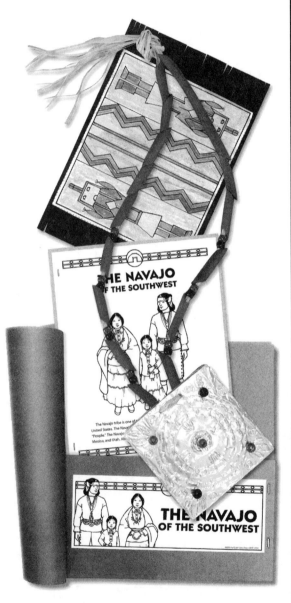

CUT AND PASTE

**Pocket Label, Shelter Stamp,
Picture Dictionary Cards**.................... **page 65**
See page 2 for information on how to prepare the
pocket label and shelter stamp. See page 10 for
information on how to prepare the picture
dictionary cards.

FACT SHEET

The Navajo .... **page 66**
Read this background information to familiarize
yourself with the Navajo. Share the information with
your students as appropriate. Incorporate library
and multimedia resources that are available.

STUDENT BOOKLET

Make a Navajo Booklet .... **pages 67–69**
See page 2 for information on how to prepare the
student booklet. Read and discuss the information
as a class. Encourage students to read their booklets
to partners or independently.

ACTIVITIES

Design a Navajo Necklace .... **pages 70 & 71**
Students may discover that they can be silversmiths
when they make a turquoise and silver Navajo
necklace.

Create a Navajo Rug .... **pages 72 & 73**
The Navajo are famous for their weavings using
colorful geometric designs. Students create their
own Navajo rug, using the art of crayon resist.

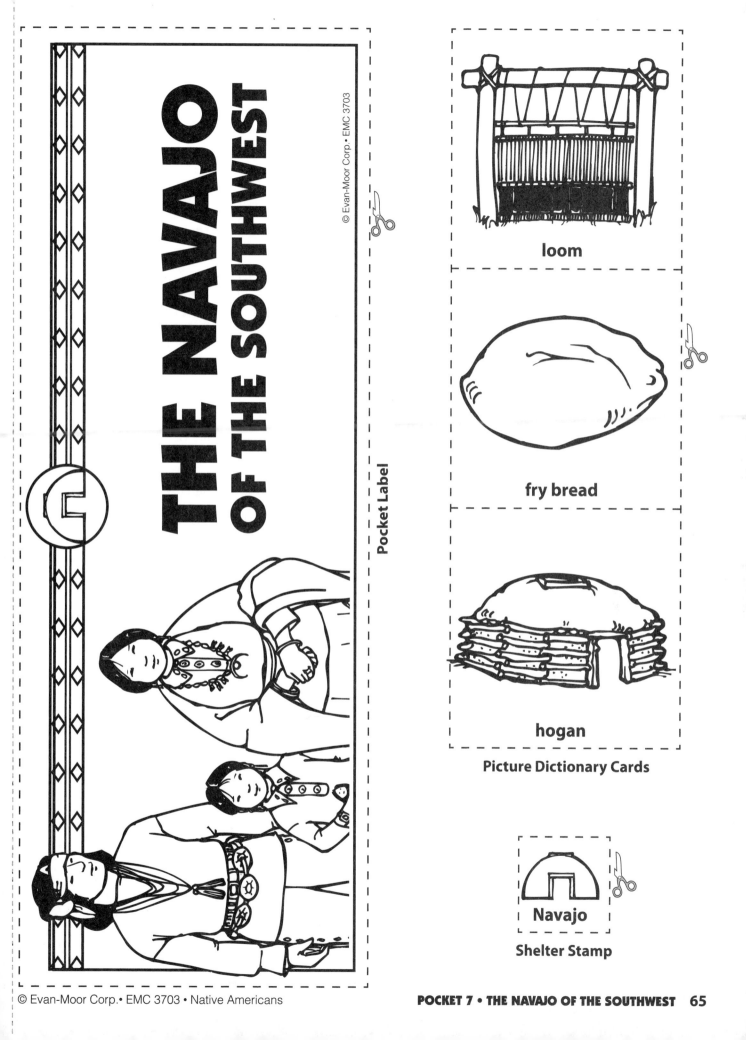

THE NAVAJO OF THE SOUTHWEST

Pocket Label

loom

fry bread

hogan

Picture Dictionary Cards

Navajo

Shelter Stamp

© Evan-Moor Corp.• EMC 3703

THE NAVAJO

INTRODUCTION

The Navajo (NAV uh hoh) tribe is one of the largest in the western United States. The Navajo lived in the canyons and mountains of Arizona, New Mexico, and Utah. About 200,000 Navajo currently live on the 28,000-square-mile (72,520 square kilometers) Navajo reservation located in the Southwest. The Navajo people call themselves the "Dineh," which means "People."

CLOTHING

Long before they had contact with European explorers, the Navajo wore clothes made from deerskin. Men often wore breechcloths and leggings, while women wore deerskin dresses. Both men and women wore moccasins.

Later on, Navajo clothing was often brightly colored. Men wore shirts and pants that ended halfway between the knee and ankle. They also wore a blanket that they wrapped across one shoulder. The Navajo highlighted their clothing with belts, bracelets, and necklaces made from silver and leather.

As time went on, women wore dresses made from wool. These dresses were often made from two blankets sewn together at the shoulders. Women also wore cradleboards so they could carry their babies on their backs.

FOOD

In spite of the hot, dry climate of the Southwest, the Navajo grew and harvested corn, potatoes, wheat, and fruits. However, sheep were the main source of food for the Navajo. The meat was added to soup or stew along with vegetables. Fry bread, made from wheat they had grown, usually accompanied the meal.

SHELTER

The Navajo built circular-shaped earth lodge houses that they called hogans, a Navajo word meaning "house." A hogan had a frame of sticks and logs that were covered with mud. A hogan consisted of one giant room that measured about 20 to 30 feet (6 to 9 meters) across. There was a smoke hole in the center of the roof. The entrance to each hogan always faced east so the Navajo could pay respect to the rising sun.

Separate from the house was a veranda called a ramada. The Navajo built each ramada from four poles and a frame. The frame was then covered with brush to provide shade.

In the summer, the Navajo often wandered with their sheep herds. When winter approached, they returned to their hogans to live. If a family member died, the hogan was abandoned and the family built a new one.

FAMILY LIFE

In the Navajo tribe, horses belonged to the men, while sheep and most other possessions belonged to the women. Navajo women spun, dyed, and wove the sheep's wool into beautiful blankets, clothing, and rugs. They incorporated many intricate designs and patterns. Navajo women used cacti and other plants, shrubs, and trees to make dye for their wool. Weaving was done outdoors on large vertical looms. Navajo women passed along their skills, traditions, and tools to their daughters. In fact, all Navajo property was passed from mother to daughter.

Navajo men were responsible for hunting, silverwork, and many ceremonial activities. Navajo silversmiths often made bridle ornaments for their horses, as well as belts, bracelets, rings, water bottles, and boxes.

Navajo men and women participated in dry painting. Dry painting was a type of sand painting used during a ceremony to help cure someone's illness. The dry painting was performed inside the hogan and often took hours to make. When the ceremony was over, the painting was destroyed because it had served its purpose.

Navajo children were raised by grandparents, aunts, uncles, and older brothers and sisters. At an early age, Navajo children learned to respect and act like their elders.

Boys learned to hunt and track animals, while girls learned to cook and weave. Both boys and girls cared for sheep, which they were told would someday belong to them.

 EMC 3703 • Native Americans • © Evan-Moor Corp.

THE NAVAJO
OF THE SOUTHWEST

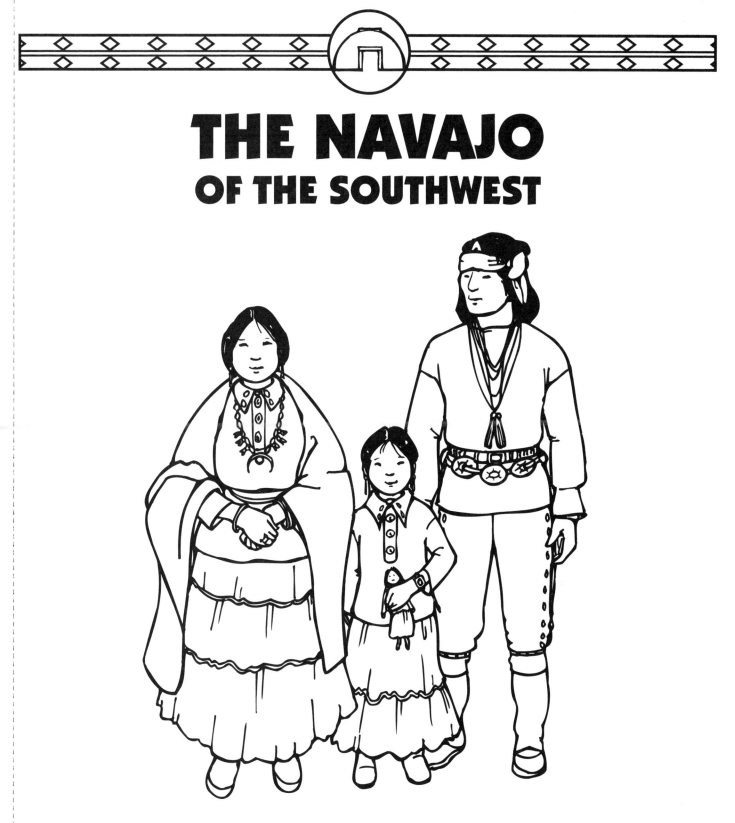

The Navajo tribe is one of the largest Native American tribes in the United States. The Navajo refer to themselves as the "Dineh," which means "People." The Navajo lived in the canyons and mountains of Arizona, New Mexico, and Utah. About 200,000 Navajo live on a Navajo reservation today.

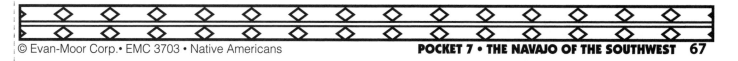

Long ago, the Navajo wore clothes made from deerskin. Later on, men wore brightly colored shirts, pants, and blankets wrapped across one shoulder. Women wore colorful dresses made from wool. They also strapped cradleboards to their backs so they could carry their babies. The Navajo also wore belts, bracelets, and necklaces made from silver, leather, and turquoise.

The Navajo planted and harvested corn, potatoes, wheat, and fruit. Sheep were their main source of food. The meat was used to make soup. Many vegetables were also added to the soup. The Navajo used the wheat they had grown to make **fry bread**. Fry bread was eaten at most meals.

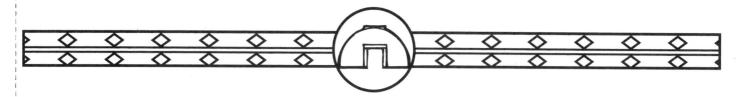

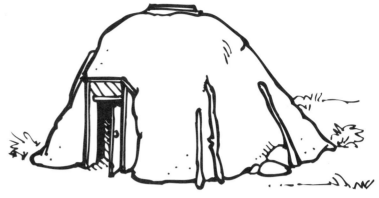

The Navajo people built lodges called **hogans**. **Hogan** is a Navajo word meaning "house." Hogans were sticks and logs packed with dirt and mud. A hogan had one giant room that measured about 20 to 30 feet (6 to 9 meters) across. There was a smoke hole in the center of the roof. The door to each hogan always faced east so the Navajo people could give thanks to the rising sun.

Navajo women used a **loom** to weave wool into beautiful blankets, clothing, and rugs. They used cacti and other plants, shrubs, and trees to make the dye that they needed. Men hunted wild animals for food and clothing. They also made silver belts, rings, and other jewelry. The Navajo made sand paintings. Sand paintings were used in ceremonies. Once a ceremony was over, the painting was destroyed.

DESIGN A NAVAJO NECKLACE

The Navajo have long been known as great silversmiths. Invite students to create a turquoise and silver Navajo-style necklace.

STEPS TO FOLLOW

1. Making the beads

   a. Pour 2 Tbsp. (30 ml) of rubbing alcohol into a plastic bag. Add several drops of blue food coloring and blend.

   b. Pour the desired amount of macaroni into the bag. Hold the bag tightly closed and shake until the macaroni is well coated.

   c. Spread out the macaroni on paper towels to dry for about 10 minutes.

2. Making the necklace

   a. Wrap the foil around the sheet of cardboard. Securely tape the foil to the back of the cardboard.

   b. Place the necklace pattern (page 71) directly on top of the foil. Use a sharpened pencil to trace over all the lines on the paper. When the pattern is lifted, the design will be imprinted on the foil. Beads may be glued to the front of the necklace, as shown.

   c. Use a hole punch to make two holes at the top of the necklace. Thread one end of the necklace cord through the holes, add the macaroni and beads, then tie the ends together.

MATERIALS

- page 71, reproduced for each student
- rubbing alcohol
- blue food coloring
- plastic bag
- paper towels
- uncooked macaroni
- 4½" square (11.5 cm) of cardboard
- 5½" square (14 cm) of aluminum foil
- beads
- string or raffia
- hole punch
- pencil
- transparent tape
- glue
- scissors

EMC 3703 • Native Americans • © Evan-Moor Corp.

DESIGN A NAVAJO NECKLACE

Use the Navajo pattern below or design your own pattern in the empty box.

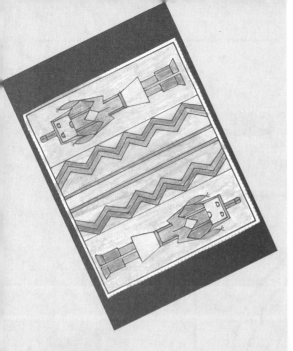

CREATE A NAVAJO RUG

The Navajo are famous for their rugs using bold colors and geometric designs. Students create their own Navajo rugs when they use a watercolor wash to accent the crayon-colored rug.

MATERIALS

- page 73, reproduced for each student
- 9" x 12" (23 x 30.5 cm) black construction paper
- crayons
- watercolor paints
- paintbrush
- container for water
- paint cloth or newspapers
- scissors
- glue

STEPS TO FOLLOW

1. If possible, use reference materials to show pictures of Navajo rugs.

2. Hand out the pattern for the rug. Students color the rug pattern using bold primary colors. When they color in the pattern, tell them to press hard to make the crayon marks dark and solid. Students should leave plenty of white space for the color wash in Step 4.

3. Cover the worktable with a paint cloth or newspapers.

4. Place the colored rugs on the table. Wet the paintbrush and dip it into the watercolor of choice. Brush across the picture of the rug, covering all the white space on the picture. This will give the picture a color wash look.

5. Allow the picture to dry.

6. Cut out the rug pattern and glue it to the black construction paper.

7. Optional: You may choose to cut a fringe on the edges of the construction paper.

EMC 3703 • Native Americans • © Evan-Moor Corp.

CREATE A NAVAJO RUG

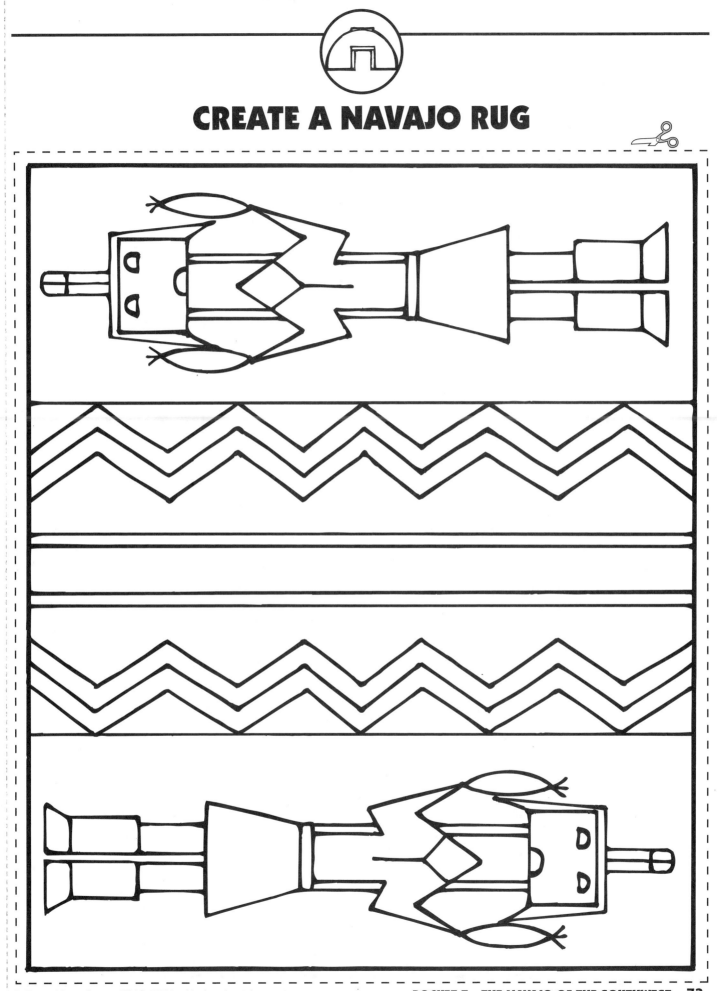

Pocket 8

THE IROQUOIS
OF THE NORTHEAST

CUT AND PASTE

**Pocket Label, Shelter Stamp,
Picture Dictionary Cards** .... **page 75**
See page 2 for information on how to prepare the
pocket label and shelter stamp. See page 10 for
information on how to prepare the picture
dictionary cards.

FACT SHEET

The Iroquois .... **page 76**
Read this background information to familiarize
yourself with the Iroquois. Share the information
with your students as appropriate. Incorporate
library and multimedia resources that are available.

STUDENT BOOKLET

Make an Iroquois Booklet .... **pages 77–79**
See page 2 for information on how to prepare the
student booklet. Read and discuss the information
as a class. Encourage students to read their booklets
to partners or independently.

ACTIVITIES

The Three Sisters .... **pages 80 & 81**
The Iroquois considered corn, beans, and squash
their "Three Sisters." Recite a poem about them
and "watch" the vegetables grow.

My Wampum Wish List .... **pages 82 & 83**
What would an Iroquois boy or girl wish for in life?
Have students ponder this question and jot down
ideas on a wampum wish list.

THE IROQUOIS OF THE NORTHEAST

Pocket Label

wampum

The Three Sisters

longhouse

Picture Dictionary Cards

Iroquois

Shelter Stamp

THE IROQUOIS

INTRODUCTION

The Iroquois (IHR uh kwoy) Confederacy was made up of five nations: the Mohawk, Oneida, Onondaga, Seneca, and Cayuga. Eventually a sixth nation, the Tuscarora, also became part of the Iroquois Confederacy. The name *Iroquois* means "People of the Longhouse." The Iroquois inhabited the northeastern woodlands of present-day New York and Quebec.

CLOTHING

Most Iroquois clothing was made from deerskin. Men often wore a pair of loose-fitting leggings and a breechcloth, which was held in place by a long belt. When the weather was cold, Iroquois men wore fringed deerskin shirts. Sometimes men wore kilts and caps covered with feathers. Most Iroquois men cut off all of their hair, except for one section that ran down the center of their scalp. This section of hair, called a roach, is known today as a "mohawk."

Iroquois women wore long deerskin skirts and leggings. In cooler weather, they wore fringed capes as blouses. Women grew their hair long and usually wore it braided. Both men and women wore moccasins. Most Iroquois clothing was decorated with colorful beads and quills.

FOOD

The Iroquois were primarily farmers, although they hunted game, fished, and gathered fruits and nuts. The three most important crops were corn, beans, and squash, which the Iroquois called "The Three Sisters." The Iroquois were able to grow 15 types of corn, 8 types of squash, and more than 60 types of beans.

In the spring, the Iroquois collected sap from maple trees to make maple syrup. Spring was also planting time. During the summer, as the crops grew, Iroquois men often caught fish. When it was harvest time, women and children picked and preserved corn, while men prepared to hunt in the mountains for deer and moose. Fall was also the time when nuts such as acorns, hickory nuts, hazelnuts, and chestnuts were plentiful. Iroquois women and children wandered through the forest and gathered nuts from the forest floor.

SHELTER

The Iroquois lived in long, narrow buildings called longhouses. An average-size longhouse was about 100 feet (30 meters) long and 20 feet (6 meters) wide. A longhouse was home to many Iroquois families belonging to the same clan.

A long hallway ran down the center of the longhouse, dividing it into two halves. Along the sides of the longhouse, Iroquois families lived in small areas. The family area was divided into two levels. On the lower level, the entire family slept together under a bearskin blanket. On the upper level, the family stored their belongings.

The Iroquois built their longhouses near riverbanks and surrounded their villages with high fences or palisades. Each day and night an Iroquois warrior guarded the village. After about 10 years, the soil was no longer as rich as it once had been. When this occurred, the Iroquois would leave their villages to search for fertile farmland and build new homes.

FAMILY LIFE

The Iroquois formed a Great Council in which all of the members were male. However, the men chosen for the Great Council were picked by the women. The purpose of the Great Council was to discuss the needs of all nations and make important decisions together.

Leaders were notified of Council meetings when strings of wampum were sent to their villages. Wampum was a collection of small beads made from shells and woven into belts.

Special ceremonies were also an important part of Iroquois life. Each August the Iroquois held the Green Corn Ceremony in order to give thanks to "The Three Sisters" for a plentiful harvest.

Children were important to the Iroquois. Babies were kept safe in cradleboards until they were two years old. Iroquois men and women often made toys for their children, such as toy birch-bark canoes and cornhusk dolls dressed in deerskin clothing. Boys learned how to hunt, trap, and fish for food. Girls learned how to plant seeds, harvest crops, cook, and make clothing.

THE IROQUOIS
OF THE NORTHEAST

The name **Iroquois** means "People of the Longhouse." The Iroquois were actually six nations combined together. The five original nations were the Mohawk, Oneida, Onondaga, Seneca, and Cayuga. Later on, the Tuscarora joined. The Iroquois lived in the area we know today as Quebec and New York.

Most Iroquois clothing was made from deerskin. In the winter, they wore fringed deerskin shirts. Sometimes men wore kilts and caps that were covered with feathers. Iroquois women wore long deerskin skirts and leggings. In the winter, they wore fringed capes as blouses. Iroquois clothing was decorated with colorful beads and quills. Both men and women wore moccasins.

The Iroquois were mostly farmers. The three most important crops were corn, beans, and squash. The Iroquois called these three crops **"The Three Sisters."** The Iroquois also hunted game, fished, and gathered fruits and nuts. In the spring, the Iroquois collected sap from maple trees and made maple syrup.

When it was harvest time, women and children picked corn and gathered nuts. Iroquois men hunted in the mountains for deer and moose.

The Iroquois built long, narrow buildings called **longhouses.** A longhouse was home to many Iroquois families. A long hallway divided the longhouse into two halves. Each family lived in a small area divided into two levels. On the upper level, they stored their belongings. On the lower level, the family slept.

The Iroquois formed a Great Council to decide important matters. Iroquois women were in charge of the village. They chose the men who would be on the Council. The women owned the property. They farmed and took care of the children. The men hunted and were good fur traders. They used beads called **wampum** for trading. Boys learned how to hunt, trap, and fish. Girls learned how to plant seeds, cook, and make clothing.

THE THREE SISTERS

Many Native American groups planted what they called "The Three Sisters," which were corn, beans, and squash. These crops were often planted together. Not only could "the sisters" be eaten fresh, but they could also be dried for future use and the corn could be ground into meal for making bread.

STEPS TO FOLLOW

1. Color and cut out "The Three Sisters" pattern. Be sure to color the "dirt" as well.

2. Fold the pattern in thirds as shown.

3. Put glue on the back of the top section of the pattern. Affix it toward the top of the construction paper.

4. Glue the bean, corn, and pumpkin seeds to the dirt just above the title.

5. Cut out the poem and glue it onto the bottom third of the construction paper.

6. Optional: Have students write about "The Three Sisters" and glue the writing paper onto the back of the construction paper. Have students learn to recite the poem.

MATERIALS

- page 81, reproduced for each student
- 6" x 9" (15 x 23 cm) construction paper
- one bean, one corn, and one pumpkin seed for each student
- crayons or marking pens
- scissors
- glue
- Optional: 5" x 8" (13 x 20 cm) writing paper

THE THREE SISTERS

Three sisters dressed all in green.
Tall Sister Corn, twisting Sister Bean.
Sister Squash wound 'round their feet.
The better they grow, the more we eat.

The Three Sisters

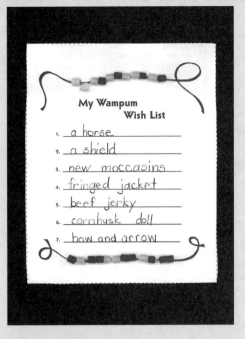

MATERIALS

- page 83, reproduced for each student
- 9" x 12" (23 x 30.5 cm) construction paper
- uncooked macaroni
- rubbing alcohol
- red and blue food coloring
- plastic bag
- paper towels
- glue
- pencil
- scissors

MY WAMPUM WISH LIST

The Iroquois often traded wampum for things they wanted or needed. Wampum was small beads made from shells and woven into strings or belts. Because purple shells were more difficult to find, purple wampum was considered to be more valuable than white wampum. Have students jot down a wampum wish list and embellish it with wampum beads.

STEPS TO FOLLOW

1. Making the beads

   a. Pour 2 Tbsp. (30 ml) of rubbing alcohol into a plastic bag. Add several drops of red and blue food coloring and blend.

   b. Pour the desired amount of macaroni into the bag. Hold the bag tightly closed and shake until the macaroni is well coated.

   c. Spread out the macaroni on paper towels to dry for about 10 minutes.

2. Making the wish list

   a. Ask students to think about what an Iroquois boy or girl might want to have. Students write down ideas on a wampum wish list (page 83).

   b. Make a design by gluing non-dyed macaroni and purple macaroni to the top and bottom of the list.

   c. Allow the glue to dry.

   d. Cut out the list and glue it to the construction paper.

   e. Share the list with classmates.

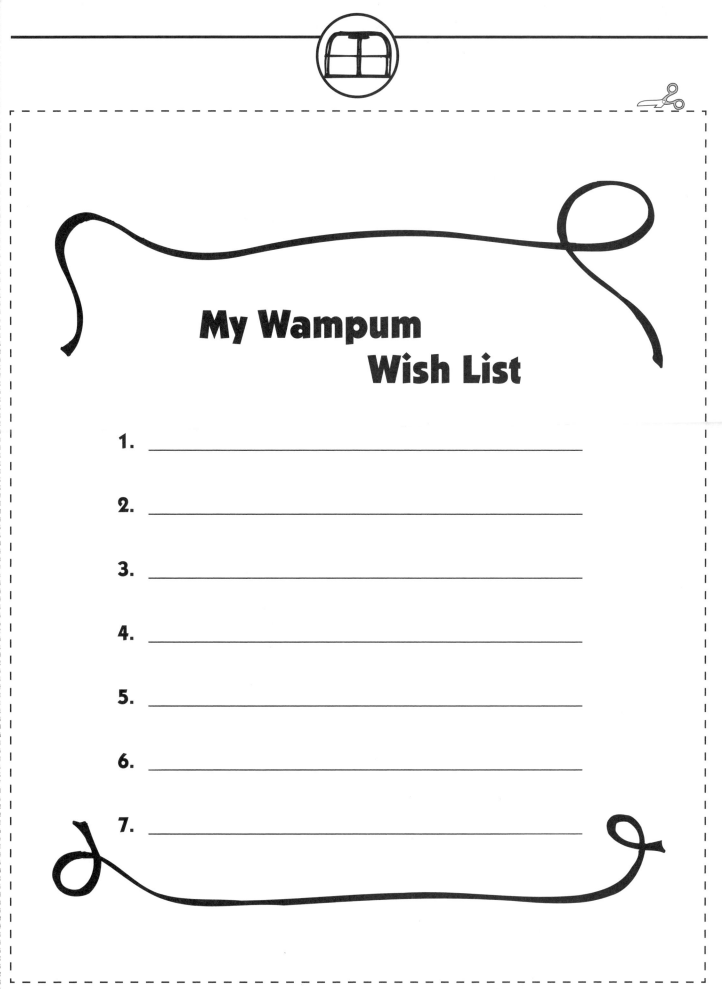

My Wampum Wish List

1. _____

2. _____

3. _____

4. _____

5. _____

6. _____

7. _____

Pocket 9

THE SEMINOLE
OF THE SOUTHEAST

CUT AND PASTE

**Pocket Label, Shelter Stamp,
Picture Dictionary Cards**.................... **page 85**
See page 2 for information on how to prepare the
pocket label and shelter stamp. See page 10 for
information on how to prepare the picture
dictionary cards.

FACT SHEET

The Seminole............................... **page 86**
Read this background information to familiarize
yourself with the Seminole. Share the information
with your students as appropriate. Incorporate
library and multimedia resources that are available.

STUDENT BOOKLET

Make a Seminole Booklet.............. **pages 87–89**
See page 2 for information on how to prepare the
student booklet. Read and discuss the information
as a class. Encourage students to read their booklets
to partners or independently.

ACTIVITIES

Wear a Seminole Headdress......... **pages 90 & 91**
Students make a Seminole headdress to wear for
a special occasion.

**How to Make Hominy
Seminole-style** .... **pages 92 & 93**
Share this recipe with students and have them write
the steps as you make this corn dish as a class.

   EMC 3703 • Native Americans • © Evan-Moor Corp.

© Evan-Moor Corp. • EMC 3703

THE SEMINOLE OF THE SOUTHEAST

Pocket Label

necklaces

hominy

chickee

Picture Dictionary Cards

Seminole

Shelter Stamp

FACT SHEET
THE SEMINOLE

INTRODUCTION

The Seminole (SEHM uh nohl) people were once part of the Creek tribe. They farmed the southern regions of what is known today as Georgia and Alabama. When European settlers arrived, some of the Creek people decided to stay behind. Others decided to move to northern and central Florida. These people became known as the Seminole, a word meaning "runaway" or "wanderer."

CLOTHING

The Seminole people wore colorful cotton clothing decorated with striped or plaid designs. Patchwork designs were often made by sewing horizontal stripes from the top to the bottom of a garment.

Seminole women wore long-sleeved blouses and skirts that touched the floor. Women also wore many necklaces made of glass beads. Seminole women often received their first necklaces when they were very young girls, adding more strings of beads as time passed. It was not uncommon for a Seminole woman to wear several pounds of beaded necklaces that reached all the way to her ears.

Seminole men wore colorful shirts and plaid turbans on their heads. They also wore breechcloths and leggings. When the weather was cold, men often wore coats with ruffles called long shirts.

FOOD

The Seminole planted corn, beans, squash, other vegetables, and fruit. They also fished and hunted, often catching alligators in the Florida swamps. On land the Seminole hunted deer, bear, raccoon, squirrel, and birds. They also gathered wild foods such as roots and potatoes.

Each family farmed its own vegetable garden, but the village also had a community garden. Everyone planted and cared for the community garden. At harvest time, each family was allotted a certain amount of food.

Corn was an important part of the Seminole diet. It was often used to make a corn dish called hominy, or it was ground into meal to make cornbread. Another popular Seminole food was sofki, a thick porridge made from dried, mashed corn.

SHELTER

The Seminole living near the Everglades built open-sided wooden huts called chickees. A chickee was built on a platform raised about 3 feet (9 meters) off the swampy ground, and it had a thatched roof constructed of palmetto leaves. The roof kept out rain, while the open sides made it possible to feel the cool breezes. The Seminole slept in hammocks and had very little furniture; they spent most of their time outdoors. Each Seminole village had a cookhouse consisting of a raised hearth. A pot of food was left to cook on the hearth for most of the day.

The Seminole who lived in northern Florida, where the land was drier, built a different type of home. Each family had two buildings. The main building had two rooms—one for sleeping and the other for cooking. The second building was a two-story building used mostly for food storage.

FAMILY LIFE

A Seminole village was made up of many families. The families in each village were related through their mothers. All women and their children belonged to the same clan.

Seminole women worked near the camp, taking care of the children, cooking, sewing, and gardening. Seminole men spent most of their time hunting, fishing, and farming. The Florida Everglades region, however, did not provide much useful farmland. Cattle were difficult to raise because the land was too swampy for grazing. Therefore, the Seminole people of this region gathered plants, fished, and hunted instead of growing crops.

In early summer, the Seminole prepared for an important festival—the Green Corn Dance. Many Seminole villages came together to celebrate the festivities by dancing, playing games, and feasting. If a naming ceremony was to be held that year, it was performed as part of the Green Corn Dance. Each Seminole boy who took part in the ceremony was given a new name. The Seminole men and boys met at the Council house, while the women prepared for the feast.

EMC 3703 • Native Americans • © Evan-Moor Corp.

THE SEMINOLE
OF THE SOUTHEAST

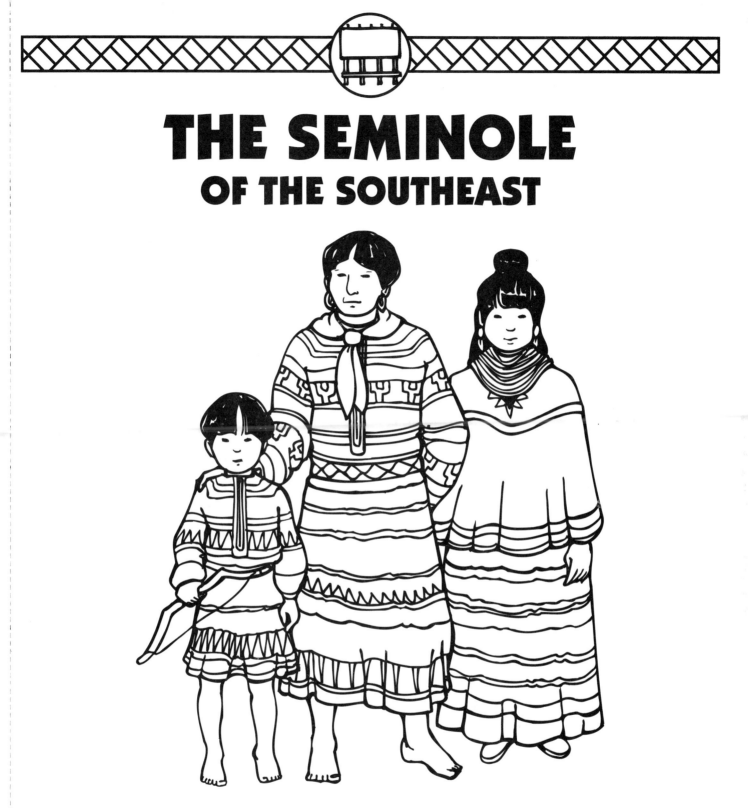

The Seminole people were once part of the Creek tribe. When European settlers arrived, some of the Creek people stayed behind. Other Creek people decided to move to Florida. The Creek that settled in Florida became known as the Seminole. **Seminole** is a word that means "wanderer" or "runaway."

The Seminole wore colorful cotton clothing. Women wore long-sleeved blouses and skirts that touched the floor. They also wore many beaded **necklaces**. Sometimes the necklaces reached from a woman's neck to her ears. Seminole men wore colorful shirts. They wore turbans, leggings, and breechcloths. When the weather was cold, men wore ruffled coats called long shirts.

The Seminole planted corn, beans, and squash. Corn was cooked to make a favorite food called **hominy**. The Seminole also fished and caught alligators in Florida swamps. They hunted deer, bear, raccoon, squirrel, and birds. Each family had its own vegetable garden. People also worked in the village garden. Everyone planted and harvested together.

Seminole people who lived in drier parts of Florida built their homes directly on the ground. The Seminole who lived in the swamps built wooden huts called **chickees**. A chickee was built on a platform 3 feet (9 meters) off the wet, muddy ground. A chickee had a roof made from palmetto leaves. A chickee had no walls. Seminole families could sit inside their chickees and feel the cool breezes. At night each person slept in a hammock inside the chickee.

Seminole women took care of the children, cooked, sewed, and worked in the garden. Seminole men hunted, fished, and farmed. Each summer the Seminole prepared for an important festival called the Green Corn Dance. People from many villages gathered. They danced, played games, ate food, and celebrated. Sometimes Seminole boys would receive new names. While the men and boys met at the Council house, the women got ready for the feast.

WEAR A SEMINOLE HEADDRESS

Students put a Seminole headdress together and imagine what it would be like to participate in a Seminole celebration.

MATERIALS

- page 91, reproduced for each student
- 9" x 12" (23 x 30.5 cm) colored construction paper
- 12 beads for each student
- scissors
- marking pens
- glue
- stapler

STEPS TO FOLLOW

1. Color the Seminole headdress pattern with marking pens.

2. Cut out the headdress pattern and glue it to a sheet of construction paper. Cut around the pattern, leaving a border of construction paper around the edges.

3. If desired, glue beads to the headdress and let it dry.

4. To make a headband, cut a long strip from construction paper. Staple one end of the strip to the headdress.

5. Place the headdress on each student's head and wrap the loose end of the headband around the back of the head. Mark the place where the other end should be stapled.

6. Staple the marked end of the headband to the headdress and cut off any extra paper. Prepare to celebrate!

WEAR A SEMINOLE HEADDRESS

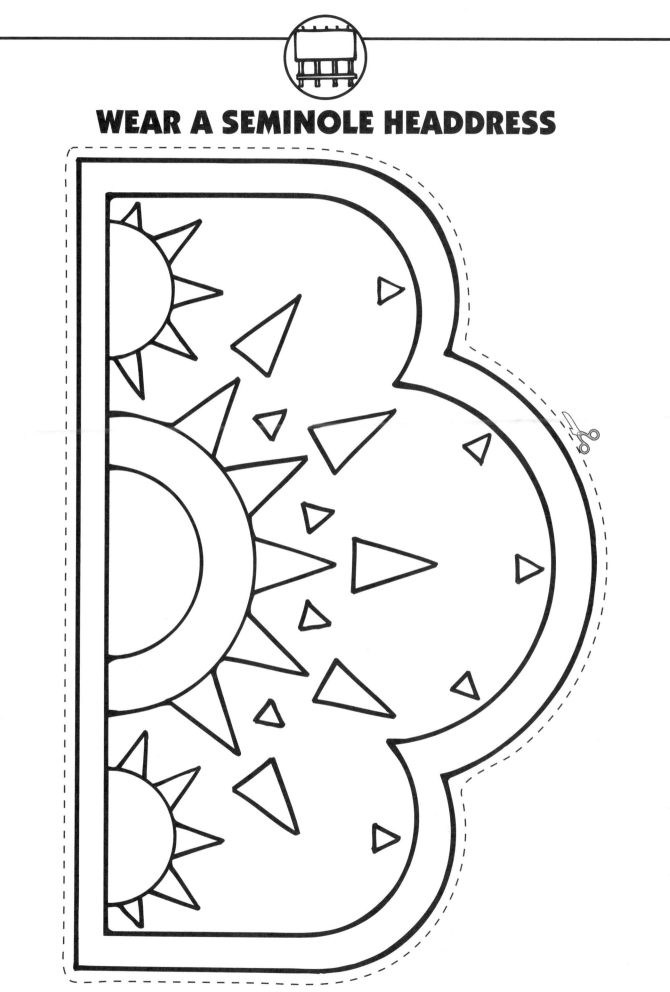

HOW TO MAKE HOMINY SEMINOLE-STYLE

Jump into cooking, while teaching students to follow a sequence of steps in a recipe at the same time.

STEPS TO FOLLOW

1. The teacher may choose to make the hominy in class, following the recipe below, or have the hominy already made for the students.

2. Have students color and cut apart the four recipe cards and cover on page 93. Discuss the order of sequence for the recipe.

3. Students glue each card to a piece of construction paper.

4. Use a hole punch to make two holes on the top of each of the five pieces of paper.

5. Use the yarn to tie them together in the proper sequence.

HOW TO MAKE HOMINY

You will need:

½ c. (80 g) dried popping corn

¾ tsp. (3 g) baking soda

1 c. (240 ml) water

1 tsp. (4.5 g) butter

pinch of salt

cooking pot

sieve

First, mix the baking soda and water together in a pot. Add the corn and set aside overnight.

Next, in the morning, place the pot on the stove. When the corn begins to boil, turn down the heat. Place the lid on the pot and let simmer for 3 hours. Then pour the corn into a sieve and let the water drain through it.

Then, place the corn in cold water and remove the popcorn hulls with your fingers.

Last, boil the corn two more times and remove any leftover hulls. Add a little butter and salt to the corn. Now you are ready to eat Seminole-style hominy!

Serves 4 (or makes enough for a spoonful for each student in class)

- page 93, reproduced for each student
- five 4" x 6" (10 x 15 cm) pieces of construction paper
- scissors
- marking pens or crayons
- hole punch
- yarn
- glue

HOMINY SEMINOLE-STYLE

How to Make Hominy

First, we mix water, baking soda, and popcorn together. We let it soak overnight.

Next, we boil the corn and then let it simmer for 3 hours. Then we pour the corn into a sieve and let it drain.

Then, we place the corn in cold water. We remove the popcorn hulls from the corn with our fingers.

Last, we boil the corn two more times and remove any leftover hulls. We add a little butter and salt to the corn. We enjoy the hominy.

Pocket 2—THE INUIT

kamiks — waterproof sealskin boots that reach up to the knees

caribou — a deer found in the Arctic and subarctic regions of North America

igluviak — a house of tightly-packed snow "bricks"; sometimes called an igloo

Pocket 3—THE TLINGIT

Chilkat robe — a fringed woven blanket worn by chiefs and nobles

potlatch hat — a hat worn at a ceremony that included a special feast and gift-giving to guests

totem pole — a pole carved and/or painted with symbols that represent a family's history

Pocket 4—THE NEZ PERCE

buckskin — a strong grayish-yellow leather made from deerskin; used in clothing

camas bulb — a sweet-tasting plant of the lily family with edible bulbs

cornhusk bag — a bag made from hemp and cornhusks; used to carry food and supplies

Pocket 5—THE MAIDU

feather bunch — a crown made from feathers and quills

seed beater — woven netting made of willow; used to knock seeds into a basket

earth lodge — a round shelter made of wood and covered with branches, reeds, and earth and built over a deep pit

Pocket 6—THE SIOUX

parfleche — a carryall made of rawhide; used to carry food and clothing

wasna — dried, pounded buffalo meat mixed with boiled animal fat and chokecherries (also called *pemmican*; similar to jerky)

tipi — cone-shaped shelter covered with buffalo hides (also spelled *tepee*)

Pocket 7—THE NAVAJO

loom — a device for interweaving sheep's wool into cloth

fry bread — a flat bread made of wheat baked in a clay oven

hogan — an earth-covered house

Pocket 8—THE IROQUOIS

wampum — strings of purple and white tubular shell beads used in clothing and for trade

The Three Sisters — the name given to beans, corn, and squash

longhouse — a shelter with a wooden frame covered with bark

Pocket 9—THE SEMINOLE

necklaces — strings of colored beads; women wore as many as 200 at a time

hominy — corn that is soaked and mashed; served as a porridge or used to make bread

chickee — an open-sided wooden hut on stilts with just a roof and floor

A LETTER FROM LONG AGO

Directions: Choose a favorite Native American group from the pockets. Pretend you are from that tribe. Write to a new friend telling about your tribe.

_____

Date

Hello _____ ,

    My name is _____ . I am _____ years old.

I am a member of the _____ .

I live in the _____ region of the United States.

My house is called a _____ .

The house is made from _____ .

My favorite food is _____ .

My clothing is made from _____ .

I help my family by _____ .

I like to _____ and _____ .

    Here is a picture I drew for you:

    I hope we can be friends. Please write back to me and tell me about your tribe.

Your new friend,

_____

MY FAVORITES

Directions: Look at all of your Native American pockets. Finish each sentence below with your favorites from all the tribes.

1. My favorite name of a Native American tribe is

   _____ .

2. My favorite kind of shelter is

   _____ .

3. My favorite kind of food is

   _____ .

4. My favorite kind of clothing is

   _____ .

5. My favorite kind of work is

   _____ .

6. My favorite playtime activity is

   _____ .

7. My favorite artwork is

   _____ .

8. My favorite animal that Native Americans hunted is

   _____ .

9. My favorite Native American name is

   _____ .

10. My favorite Native American name I would call myself is

   _____ .

 EMC 3703 • Native Americans • © Evan-Moor Corp.